Unity in Diversity

Fifty Years

of

Cultural Integration

ISBN 0-916985-00-8

UNITY IN DIVERSITY

FIFTY YEARS

OF

CULTURAL INTEGRATION

Cultural Integration Fellowship
Golden Anniversary Volume
1951-2001

Edited by Vern Haddick

Cultural Integration Fellowship
San Francisco

CONTENTS

PART I: THE CULTURAL INTEGRATION FELLOWSHIP AND INTEGRALISM

PART II: TRIBUTES

PART III: A ROUND OF POETRY

PART IV: SELECTED ACADEMIC PAPERS

PART I

THE CULTURAL
INTEGRATION FELLOWSHIP
AND INTEGRALISM

INTRODUCTION

When more than fifty percent of newly-established businesses close during their first year, and the likelihood of young cultural organizations reaching a first anniversary is perhaps even smaller, it is exciting to find the Cultural Integration Fellowship, which was founded in San Francisco, in 1951, celebrating its golden anniversary with stamina and mettle.

But then the Fellowship has been doing unexpected things since its inception. It was built upon the conviction (unusual in the United States at that time, and still) that each individual being is a manifestation of the Unity of Being, a moment in the development of Spirit, a fragment of the Consciousness that pervades all things. Accordingly, a human life achieves fulfillment and feels meaningful to the degree that it expresses the richest development of which it is capable. And true development involves not only personal unfoldment, but an active participation in promoting a more loving and spiritually whole world around us. For fifty years the two remarkable founders of the Fellowship, and several generations of members, have pursued such goals together.

The present volume of writings by the founding president and past and present members includes a short history of the noteworthy institution, and essays and poems that express some of the personal growth and shared culture that the Fellowship has nurtured throughout its first half-century.

1951-2000
A Short History
of the
Cultural Integration Fellowship
by Vern Haddick

An East-West Deity

Durga, the major Hindu goddess who embodies one form of Sakti, or feminine cosmic energy, became more well-known in the United States after the middle of the twentieth century. Among the first groups to honor her here with a Durga Puja festival was the Cultural Integration Fellowship of San Francisco.

In northeastern India, Durga's homeland, her festival lasts for nine days, during which time a special image of the goddess is created from clay, worshipped, celebrated with processions and public and private festivities, and finally immersed in water to return to her primal condition. In the United States, at the Fellowship, the observance fills one evening of ritual and communal celebration, after which the beautiful painted representation of Durga is returned to her archival rest for another year.

To paraphrase the priest-celebrant of the Durga-Puja at the Fellowship, Ramen Chakrabarti:

Of course Durga came from India and brought along her traditions too. But she found different situations and needs here in faster-paced, industrialized Western culture. So the ways of worshipping her had to be acculturated and modified somewhat. As have we too, here in the West, through learning about and participating with Durga's powerful and unique energy. Meeting each other—learning through dialogue and sharing—reaching new and richer wholeness: that's Cultural Integration!

An East-West Partnership

Like Durga, Haridas and Bina Chaudhuri came to San Francisco from northeastern India at the start of the 1950s. Like the goddess, they too have been for fifty years a notable energy that contributes to the unification of the world's diverse knowledge and cultures.

Both Dr. and Mrs. Chaudhuri were born in Calcutta during the first quarter of the twentieth century. They were educated in colleges there and at the University of Calcutta. It was still the period of English dominion, and as they took degrees in the field of philosophy, they faced the inevitable challenge of clarifying and harmonizing the mixed heritage of Eastern and Western ways of thought and customs that impacted their lives. However, what may have begun at the personal level soon took on wider dimensions.

Haridas Chaudhuri became professor of logic, philosophy, and religion at several Colleges in Bengal, then chairperson of the philosophy department at Krishnagar. His doctoral dissertation on integral idealism expressed deep understanding of

10

the lifework of Sri Aurobindo, the Indian sage and leader who had both worked for India's independence and elaborated a vision of complementary Eastern and Western spiritual and cultural values. Dr. Chaudhuri became an outstanding member of the new generation of philosophers in India and helped to organize and guide the Sri Aurobindo movement there. During his time in Calcutta, he published his first important study, *Sri. Aurobindo: Prophet of Life Divine.* Sri Aurobindo, shortly before his death, and in response to an inquiry from Professor Frederic Spiegelberg of Stanford University, recommended Haridas Chaudhuri to become professor of Indian and comparative philosophy and religious studies at the newly founded American Academy of Asian Studies in San Francisco. Dr. Chaudhuri accepted the invitation, took a leave of five years from Krishnagar College, and arrived in California in March, 1951.

Bina Chakrabarti and Haridas Chaudhuri were married in 1941. Subsequently she completed her degree in philosophy, studied and became an accomplished performer of Tagore songs, and fulfilled the many duties of a wife in India during the subsequent ten years there. When Haridas Chaudhuri left for San Francisco, she and their daughters Rita and Shipra remained behind, until the four members of the family were reunited in California in July, 1952.

Upon his arrival in the United States, Dr. Chaudhuri begun to give talks to interested groups of persons on philosophy, religion, and the practical applications of spiritual resources to life in the contemporary Western world. In addition, he was also teaching at the American Academy, lecturing on occasions at Stanford University and San Francisco State College, participating in panel discussions by

11

faculty members of the Academy that were broadcast from radio station KPFA in Berkeley.

An Intercultural Organization

Through his teaching and work with students at the American Academy, Dr. Chaudhuri was part of an academic, degree program community; but he also wanted to meet, learn from, and teach a wider cross-section of Americans. Believing strongly in the development of mutual understanding between cultures, he worked actively to bridge the gap between the technological, rational-oriented expertise of the West (especially as manifested in advanced American society) and the philosophical, spiritual heritage of the East (especially as found in the long rich tradition of Hindu culture). Opportunities developed soon after his arrival.

Brief articles in newspapers that announced his presence in San Francisco, and launching his classes at the Academy, led to invitations from persons who wanted to meet and learn from him. He was equally ready to accept, as another way to get to know and understand his new cultural environment through first-hand experience. Before long other small groups of interested persons began to ask Dr. Chaudhuri to speak or teach them on particular subjects. Thus came together a number of the early supporters of Dr. Chaudhuri's work outside the Academy: Rudolph Schaffer (of the Schaffer School of Design); Olive Cowell (who taught international relations at San Francisco State College); Howard Thurman (leader of the Fellowship Church of All People); Mr. and Mrs. Charles Gruenhagen (of American Box Corporation); Walter Johnson (of American Forest Products Corporation); and Judith Tyberg (of the East-West Center in Los Angeles).

12

Soon he began to give more formally organized lectures on a regular schedule at the Rudolph Schaffer School. During this first year that he was here, the Cultural Integration Fellowship was founded as a venue for dialogue and learning between the world's cultures, a center at which various traditions could speak for themselves, dialogue, and learn through sharing experiences of their religions, philosophical beliefs, and arts. The approach at the Fellowship from the beginning was to stimulate direct interpersonal and intercultural learning.

Dr. Chaudhuri chose for it the name of Cultural Integration Fellowship to underline its approach of presenting the spiritual and cultural viewpoints of different cultures.

After functioning on an informal basis for several months, the Fellowship was formally incorporated in June 1951 as an independent, nonprofit, nondenominational religious and educational organization in California. Dr. Chaudhuri chose for it the name of Cultural Integration Fellowship to underline its approach of presenting the spiritual and cultural viewpoints of different cultures, eastern and western, northern and southern, in order to bring the peoples and nations of the world closer together in mutual understanding and cooperation.

When the rest of the family arrived, the Chaudhuris established their first, temporary family home in quarters at the Rudolph Schaffer School of Design on Union Street.

Fellowship Purposes and Practices

From its founding and throughout its first fifty years three purposes have provided energy and focus for the Fellowship's activities:

- *Stimulating and developing intercultural growth and harmony.* From the perennial insight that one universal energy manifests through the forms and traditions expressed by different peoples worldwide, comes commitment to honor and benefit from the diversity of all cultural expressions: philosophies and religions, literatures, behaviors, arts.

- *Exploring the universal spiritual values that underlie all human life.* From realizing that human beings are essentially spiritual beings, comes the quest to identify and nurture the authentic religious experience as it has been expressed in ancient and modern world traditions. Nonsectarian religious observances help to make these spiritual values accessible and tangible.

- *Incorporating universal cultural and spiritual values into human relations and daily life.* Promoting creative self-fulfillment through establishing contact with the spiritual center of the Self, and through exposing the latent harmony of personal and interpersonal living, give focus to the many ways in which the Fellowship has reached out to its members and the wider world.

Expanding Activities at the Fellowship

Mrs. Chaudhuri's arrival in San Francisco opened a cycle of new intercultural activities at the

14

Fellowship. In addition to the lectures and discussions that Dr. Chaudhuri had been providing already, further offerings and events began to explore the principles of creative self-fulfillment as related to daily living and interpersonal exchanges.

There were demonstrations and classes in cooking and flower-arranging, and the dress from various traditions was represented among the membership. The excitement of learning first-hand from persons who had been lifelong practitioners helped to fill such classes as Mrs. Chaudhuri's on Indian cookery, which are still remembered fondly many years later. Other offerings combined dance recitals with classes in Indian and other non-Western dance, to offer a new, integrated physical-intellectual-spiritual experience of life in different cultures. The intent and focus was to learn about other persons and cultures, not abstractly, but directly; to allow cultures to express themselves through performers and well-known scholars of many backgrounds.

Recitals and performances of music from various traditions served a similar purpose. Sometimes the artists came from abroad (for example, Ustad Alla Rakha, Zakir Hussain, and Aashish Khan), and on occasion they made their first American appearances at the Fellowship. Other times the event crystallized out of energies present within the membership: Lillian Foote organized and led a chorus that frequently performed a variety of music during Sunday morning services, and Lyne Duchamp shared recitals of European arias and songs. Professor Chang was secured to lecture and lead classes on Chinese brush painting, so helping to provide voice for another rich cultural tradition.

Rudolph Schaffer, too, continued to be a rich resource for the arts of the Fellowship down the years. Beyond providing an actual first home in the United States, for both the organization and the Chaudhuris, he enriched the Fellowship with his professional expertise and contacts, and he remained a loyal and generous supporter in many other practical ways throughout his very long life.

Demonstrations and classes in meditation, tai-chi, and several schools of yoga provided yet another channel for experiencing integrated development of the self from perspectives of different non-Western traditions, again taught by practitioners from the tradition itself. At the same time, lectures and workshops on Western psychological approaches encouraged dialogue between Western and other ways of handling issues in personal and interpersonal living.

Two Homes

Within a couple of years after the Chaudhuris had arrived and taken up their work in the Bay Area, the American Academy of Asian Studies began to suffer from financial and administrative difficulties from which it never recovered. Accordingly, when Aushim, the Chaudhuris' third child was born, the family was considering returning to India and to Dr. Chaudhuri's tenured teaching position there. However, the Fellowship was growing and flourishing, and their desire to continue their pioneering work in the Bay Area was strong. A timely and substantial weight was added to the balance when Mr. and Mrs. Gruenhagen and Walter Johnson, who had become committed students and early supporters of Dr. Chaudhuri's work, helped to provide funds to buy the building at 3494 21st Street in San Francisco as a home for the Chaudhuris, the Fellowship, and its growing activities.

For several years the family, the professional activities, and the Fellowship activities of Sunday lectures and midweek meetings and classes, fit comfortably into the two-storied wooden home. But sometimes the crowds overflowed the large comfortable living room that was located just inside the front door, into the adjacent hallway and staircase; that was a portent of the need for additional space that would develop by the mid-1950s.

So, again with encouragement and assistance from the Gruenhagens and Walter Johnson, in 1956 a new home was purchased for the Fellowship at 2650 Fulton Street, beside Golden Gate Park in San Francisco. The Chaudhuri family remained in their home on 21st Street, and the Fulton Street building was dedicated and occupied as headquarters for the Fellowship on January 6, 1957.

The scope of activities continued to expand. The centerpiece remained the Sunday morning talks on spiritual, philosophical, and cultural topics that Dr. Chaudhuri delivered each week. Some of them were transcribed and reproduced for distribution. Others that comprised series on related subjects were developed into several of Dr. Chaudhuri's earlier books, such as *Philosophy of Integralism* (1954), *The Integral Philosophy of Sri Aurobindo* (1960), and *Mastering the Problems of Living* (1968).

Each Tuesday evening Dr. Chaudhuri led study classes, and soon, authorized by the California State Department of Education, the Fellowship began to offer certificates to qualified students who had met the required standards of attendance at a specified number of classes and produced worthy research papers. Thursday evenings were usually reserved for events with distinguished guest speakers from across the United States and abroad: academic colleagues of Dr. Chaudhuri, or notable scholars and religious leaders and creative personalities from India and other countries, among them Lama Govinda, Framroze Bode, Judith Tyberg, Ajit Mookerjee, and Amiya Chakravarti. Other nights of the week accommodated continuing classes on the practice of meditation as a discipline for spiritual and personal growth; yoga or tai-chi, as a vehicle for psycho-spiritual integration; and, from time to time, continuing psychological work groups. Weekends were often occupied with special workshops or celebrations, and social parties and membership meetings, in addition to the regular Sunday morning lectures.

Dr. Chaudhuri also carried the application of Fellowship principles forward into the realm of daily life by offering personal guidance on self-development to individuals and groups, and by conducting nonsectarian religious services such as ceremonies of marriage, baptisms, and memorial services. Such events were particularly helpful to younger persons struggling at the time of the 1950s and 1960s to find meaningful replacements for traditional rituals; fifty years later some individuals still remember appreciatively the comfortable new fit of the intercultural approach.

When the Fellowship moved into the building on Fulton Street, it established a small residential section upstairs ("The Ashram") to accommodate a few members, students, or guests from abroad, who sought facilities for harmonious and constructive living in an atmosphere of quiet, peace, and freedom. Established as it was in the mid-1950s, "the Ashram" was one of the earliest intentional spiritually-oriented living communities to function in the Bay Area after the Second World War, before such groups became more common in the 1960s. The Ashram on Fulton Street was the first landing-spot in the United States for several distinguished visitors from India, and through the years it has also provided housing for graduate students from the California Institute of Asian (later "Integral") Studies.

Beyond the Fellowship Premises

Dr. Chaudhuri's name and work at the Fellowship soon attracted attention from beyond San Francisco, and calls for his participation in a variety of events followed. Beginning in summer 1953 he conducted periodic seminars for a group at Sedona, Arizona, which soon was organized as the Crescent Moon Branch Center of the Cultural Integration Fellowship, and co-directed by Nicholas and Lois Duncan. For a number of years following, the summer retreats held there were important intercultural and spiritual events for the region of northern Arizona, as well as a welcome break in the desert for the Chaudhuri family.

In-June 1955 Dr. Chaudhuri headed the reception committee when the Indian community of northern California honored V.K. Krishna Menon, leader of the Indian delegation to the United Nations, at the Sheraton Palace Hotel; a couple of years later he contributed his experience and expertise at the meetings of the U.S. National Commission for UNESCO, held in San Francisco in 1957. In January 1962 he gave the opening address, entitled "Ancient Hinduism in the Modern World," at the Parliament of World Religions, held at the University of Oregon. Later that same year he was speaker at the Pacific Philosopher's Conference and the Buddhists' Conference, both held at Asilomar.

While teaching, lecturing, and guiding, Dr. Chaudhuri also produced a steady stream of writings, not only as books issued by the Fellowship and other publishers, but also as articles in such international journals as *Philosophy East and West, Pacific Forum, The Calcutta Review,* and *United Asia.* Because of his scholarship, independent scholars from across the country and abroad came to study with him, and various universities sent students to pursue projects under his guidance.

> *Haridas and Bina Chaudhuri's lives also served in an informal way as a model of successful bicultural living.*

Because they were among the earliest arrivals from India to take up professional life in the United States, Haridas and Bina Chaudhuri's lives also served in an informal way as a model of successful bicultural living for the emergent Indian-American community in the Bay Area. That the Chaudhuris had succeeded in bringing together the two worlds of experience and were contributing richly to American life, provided encouragement—as well as some more practical support when needed—to others who came after. Mrs. Chaudhuri responded with good humor to one of my questions during an interview before I undertook this history:

> How I adjusted myself, leaving my family back home, was quite a challenge. It was a

struggle to adapt to the very different culture here. I guess, when other Indian women experienced similar problems, their husbands said, "If Mrs. Chaudhuri can do it, then you can do it too," and they tried.

Reviewing the productivity that issued from the buildings on Dolores and Fulton Streets one wonders where they found the energy to sustain so many activities!

Human Resources Tapped

As many and varied opportunities became available at the two Fellowship homes, many individuals became involved, helping to support and carry through work. As president, Dr. Chaudhuri organized and worked with a committed board of directors and advisory board that in these earlier years included Esther Weissman, Edith Reames, Vina Armstrong, Charles Gruenhagen and Walter Johnson, Charles Forester, Lillian Foote, Rudolph Schaffer, Pitirim Sorokin, Leo Nordquist, Jane Taylor, and Nicholas and Lois Duncan.

Mrs. Chaudhuri was indefatigable and endlessly resourceful in finding and organizing practical supports, coordinating schedules, overseeing resources, and attracting persons of unique abilities who generously gave much time and effort to the flourishing operations. Among many others, several special persons may represent the larger crowd: Lyne Duchamp, who served as welcoming hostess at Sunday meetings; Lillian Foote, who provided spectacular floral arrangements for lectures and events through thirty years, and hosted gatherings in her home on Marina Boulevard; Archana Chakrabarti and Gladys Nordquist, who often expanded

Mrs. Chaudhuri's hands to six when crises arose; Paul Herman, who became especially helpful in the educational projects that developed in the late 1960s; Sandra Kepler and Bahman Shirazi, who developed the Fellowship library and worked tirelessly as administrative assistants; and Richard Teich, who preserved taped records of meetings and lectures, and later moved the Fellowship into newer areas of advancing technology.

The three Chaudhuri children, throughout their youth and even more so after they reached adulthood, contributed steady and generous support to the organization's success. Daughters Rita and Shipra helped with many administrative and practical functions, week after week and decade after decade, including the activities connected with the fiftieth anniversary. And Aushim, the musician, not only performed for many occasions and events, but also arranged for professional associates such as Zakir Hussain to give benefit concerts for the Fellowship over many years.

As this mere listing of a few names suggests, the persons drawn to the Fellowship came from diverse backgrounds; they illustrate the success of the organization in kindling dialogue and learning between cultures at the very personal level. The Nordquists, the Gruenhagens, and Miss Duchamp came from western European roots. Mrs. Foote and Miss Kepler came to the Bay Area after earlier lives spent in the eastern United States (several decades apart in time). The Chakrabartis, like the Chaudhuris, were born in India; and Mr. Shirazi spent his youth in Teheran.

A high percentage of Fellowship participants and supporters seemed to be drawn into involvement through their deep belief in the organization's three fundamental purposes. In return, the Fellowship provided an exceptionally supportive and humane environment in which latent talents could be developed and used to personal and group benefit. A catalog of illustrations, almost as long as the list of Fellowship members, could be given here, but two or three examples may serve. First, Mrs. Chaudhuri herself. In India her lifestyle centered in academic circles and as head of her family household. On coming to San Francisco those commitments still held; but in addition she became co-founder of a growing spiritual and educational center, business and personnel coordinator for the organization, and even chauffeur for Dr. Chaudhuri and other Fellowship members in need of transportation over Bay Area streets and freeways.

Mrs. Foote, after a career as an educator, came to the Fellowship "on an Easter Sunday morning" and "listened to what I thought was the most moving Easter talk that I had ever heard." Hooked, throughout the ensuing thirty years she became a living example of the message delivered that day: that "the great mission of one's life is to fashion the raw material of the soul and transform it into a thing of beauty." She provided music, flowers, and food to the membership; financial and strategic guidance as member of the boards of governors of the Fellowship and the California Institute of Asian (Integral) Studies; and finally moral and spiritual inspiration to several generations of Fellowship participants.

I came to the Fellowship at about the time I had finished my doctoral studies in psychology at a major university, and I then and felt so disenchanted with the conventional academic world that I was ready to become a landscape gardener. Instead, I was challenged and encouraged to become the library director and a faculty member at the newly-organized Institute (the expanded educational component of the Fellowship), where I spent the richest twenty-five years of my professional life.

> *The great mission of one's life is to fashion the raw material of the soul and transform it into a thing of beauty.*

Guided by the vision of finding and giving mutual support among "like souls," the Fellowship seemed to be at the leading edge of a way of thinking about interpersonal relations that was to come into its own about two decades later: that the influence of a "family of choice" is often equally important as heritage from one's "family of birth."

Lectures and Workshops

During the first twelve years Dr. Chaudhuri carried most of the responsibility for the Sunday morning talks. They covered a wide range of topics within the disciplines of philosophy, spirituality, and cultural studies, invariably treated with the main view of promoting intercultural understanding and cooperation. Some of them were shaped into articles and books that he published. Others were included in several posthumous volumes. Many others are preserved as archival or published tape recordings. Together they convey the experience of a rich and highly-trained intelligence speaking with remarkable poise, warmth, and alert presence. The publications,

24

tapes, and memories of persons who attended his lectures all attest to his fine rapport with his audience, his ability to develop an insight that "expanded your consciousness and made you hungry for more." He spiced his talks with appropriate stories drawn from many traditions; his stories often caused his hearers to join with him in laughing with joy at the many ways the great creative impulse manifests throughout the universe.

Occasionally there were shared lectures, as when Framroze Bode spoke one morning out of his own background on "Zen and Tibetan Mysticism," or when Judith Tyberg discussed "Sri Aurobindo: the Great Reconciler of East and West." From early years it was a tradition to honor the joint birthdays of Sri Aurobindo and Indian independence in August; and often the birthday of the mystic poet and sage Rabindranath Tagore was celebrated in May. For such events there were sometimes speakers from the other side of the continent or abroad. Two examples will need to suffice.

On May 11, 1961 the birthday centenary of Tagore was celebrated at the Fellowship, in cooperation with the Consulate General of India in San Francisco, and included a recital of classical Hindu dance by Shivaram, one of its most famous exponents.

And from August 15-20 in 1972 a six-day program was co-presented by the Fellowship, Lone Mountain College, and the Consulate General of India, to celebrate the birth centenary of Sri Aurobindo and the twenty-fifth anniversary of India's independence. The opening session at the Palace of Fine Arts included talks by Dr. Chaudhuri, Mr. S.K. Saha, the Education Consul of India in San Francisco, Rammurti Mishra, and the Pulitzer Prize winning science writer Gobind Behari Lal. Several sessions at Lone Mountain College during the next days examined in detail the vision and philosophy of Sri Aurobindo and culminated in a panel discussion on the "Integral View of Man" by Dr. Chaudhuri, Alan Watts, and Ira Progoff, the founder of Dialogue House and the Intensive Journal trainings. The last sessions moved to the Fellowship building, where Dr. Progoff spoke about the Intensive Journal process and led several exercises to expand Self-awareness and Self-actualization. (For a number of years Dialogue House used the tape of those all-day sessions as an important tool in training Intensive Journal consultants.)

One Sunday morning in spring 1963, Dr. Chaudhuri had almost finished his lecture on "The Image of Man," when he excused himself as feeling unwell, and fell as he was leaving the platform. Dr. Charles Forester, a member of the board, was present and gave emergency treatment until Dr. Chaudhuri reached the hospital.

After his recovery, Dr. Chaudhuri realized it was not wise to resume the practice of speaking every Sunday. He reduced his schedule to alternate Sundays, and the series of intervening talks were given by the distinguished East-West scholars James Plaugher, Framroze Bode, and Swami Kriyananda. Others, such as Anil Sarkar and Lama Tarthang Tulku, appeared less frequently as guest lecturers.

It was not long, however, before the time was freed for Dr. Chaudhuri to become committed to an aspect of the Fellowship work even larger than weekly talks on spiritual development: the educational program was moving toward establishment of the California Institute of Asian Studies.

The California Institute of Asian Studies

As Mrs. Chaudhuri summarized, "The whole history of Cultural Integration Fellowship has a scholarly, academic overlay as a part of its story." From the beginning, Dr. Chaudhuri brought to the Fellowship his own high academic standards in his balanced, stimulating talks and in the regular classes that he began to teach there in early years. As soon as possible, he secured approval for the granting of diplomas and certificates from the State of California Department of Education. Next came authorization by the Board of Education to award certificates to students who had taken a certain sequence of classes and written acceptable research papers. A certain number of the members chose to do so. Classes, lectures by distinguished speakers, and cultural learning through music, dance, and other experiential events, came to constitute the "educational wing" of Fellowship activities.

Accordingly, it is not surprising that by the mid-1960s some of the certificate-holders began to ask for further academic opportunities. About the same time, the American Academy of Asian Studies reached its nadir, and a group of Dr. Chaudhuri's students urged him to help them find a way to gain academic degrees in a nationally accredited institution that had academic, spiritual, and intercultural orientation. Much soul-searching, research, and consultation followed; but in the end, with the wholehearted approval of the Fellowship's board, Haridas and Bina Chaudhuri became co-founders of the new California Institute of Asian Studies, as an expansion of the educational activities of the Fellowship. The school was founded upon the same philosophical assumptions as the Fellowship; the chief difference was one of focus. At the Fellowship, the lens of spirituality was invoked to examine reality and human activities; at the California Institute, the highest academic standards and practices were to be the criteria.

> *Haridas and Bina Chaudhuri*
> *became cofounders of the new*
> *California Institute of Asian Studies.*

The California Institute was founded and began to offer classes under approval from the California State Department of Education in 1968. The Chaudhuris moved into newly-built quarters at the back of their home on 21st Street at Dolores; the school established its offices and classrooms, and its first library in the original areas of the building. From the first classes were received with excitement, and enrollment by degree-oriented students grew steadily, to such extent that by fall 1969 the board and the Chaudhuris decided that the entire property at 3494 21st Street should be rented for use of the Institute, which needed one unified building for its activities. So the Chaudhuris moved out and found a new home nearby at 360 Cumberland Street (which they also opened to Institute and Fellowship events on occasion).

During the first year Dr. Chaudhuri taught most of the core classes in the curriculum, even as he assembled a group of established scholars, from East and West, to offer comparative studies in philosophy, psychology, religions, and cultures. It was the policy to have cultural studies and languages taught by scholars who had been "born and brought up in those systems." In 1969, too, Dr. Chaudhuri asked Paul Herman, a psychotherapist from the East Bay who held degrees in both academic Western psychology, and comparative East-West philosophy and psychology (under Dr. Chaudhuri's tutelage), to join the faculty and help to teach the popular classes in philosophy and psychology. That hire proved a most auspicious one for the Institute's future.

When the decision was made to secure accreditation of the school from the Western Association of Schools and Colleges (the regional unit in the national accreditation system), many new operations and facilities had to be developed. A board of directors for the Institute was established, with Leo Nordquist and Jane Taylor as key members and successive chairpersons. An office and support staff had to be found, trained, and inspired. Mrs. Chaudhuri moved skillfully into this part of operations (in addition to continuing her full load of activities at the Fellowship and serving as secretary to President Haridas Chaudhuri); Lillian Foote volunteered a generous share of time each week to help her. Also, a library had to be created to support serious academic work. From 1968 until 1974—when the Fellowship and Institute were formally separated as part of gaining accreditation for the California Institute of Asian Studies—the Fellowship as an organization, and many members as individuals, gave crucial financial, moral, and practical support to the new graduate school. The Fellowship contributed to the rental cost of the building on 21st Street and donated its library (Dr. Chaudhuri did the same) to establish the core of the needed collection of books. When the school required larger space from time to time, the

Fellowship provided it at the Fulton Street building; there Institute major events and graduations, as well as larger classes and workshops, were held for many years.

> *Paul Herman founded the psychology training programs and launched them in 1973.*

During the early 1970s, classes of Dr. Chaudhuri's and Paul Herman's that had a specifically psychological bent were in great demand., and students began to ask for fuller training in a truly East-West psychology. Paul Herman proposed that the Institute develop and offer an Integral Counseling Psychology training program which could lead to state licenses for its graduates. Dr. Chaudhuri gave his enthusiastic support and obtained approval from the board of directors. Consulting with Dr. Chaudhuri and other professionals, Paul Herman founded the psychology training programs and launched them in 1973. They resulted in an immediate spurt of growth in enrollment at the school, and for at least the next twenty years these programs produced the largest blocks of income and graduates among the Institute's academic offerings. Out of need for a training site for the student counselor-trainees, Paul Herman also developed the first of the Institute's counseling centers and directed it for a number of years, as part of the Integral Counseling Psychology program. The program and Counseling Center were particular strengths of the Institute that were cited in reports of the accreditation teams that visited the school regularly during the years of candidacy status; the team-members expressed special enthusiasm about the effective and new application of an intercultural orientation in the field of mental health.

Throughout the early 1970s great effort went into developing resources, personnel, faculty, and programs at the California Institute of Asian Studies. By 1975 the board of directors and consultants felt that it was time to ask the Western Association of Schools and Colleges for a full accreditation visit. However, in June before the scheduled visit took place, Dr. Chaudhuri passed away very suddenly from a heart attack, and the full accreditation was delayed.

The boards at both the Fellowship and the California Institute of Asian Studies asked Mrs. Chaudhuri to step into the office of acting president. She did so, and led organizations that she had co-founded into successful new achievements.

The Fellowship's Twenty-Fifth Anniversary

Becoming second president of the Fellowship—in addition to the other major responsibilities that devolved upon her—Mrs. Chaudhuri set about evoking and regrouping the forces within herself and the membership that would carry the organization through the next twenty-five years to accomplishments as significant as those of the first decades under the leadership of Haridas Chaudhuri.

The twenty-fifth anniversary was celebrated on March 28, 1976, with Professor Vasant Joshi as guest speaker to discuss the topic of universal religion. However, Mrs. Chaudhuri's part in the

31

morning's program was most significant in revealing the deep roots that would nourish activities to come. I would like to reconstruct the gist of her short talk here from the draft that she provided:

We are celebrating today the twenty-fifth anniversary of the Cultural Integration Fellowship, but it is not my intention to make a speech this morning. My purpose is to state briefly, to reaffirm, the basic ideals of our Fellowship, and to say a few words about how it all started. It is also good once in a while to rededicate ourselves to the spiritual ideal of life.

Let me state briefly the three basic ideals of the Fellowship: the concepts of universal religion, cultural harmony, and creative or constructive self-development. First, the universal religion. Dr. Joshi, our honored guest speaker, is going to discuss the meaning of universal religion; so I will not go into that. The second basic concept is cultural harmony. We all know that the great need of our present time is for cooperation among the different peoples of the world, for better understanding of each other so that we can work together toward the fulfillment of the common goals of humanity. But we find all kinds of obstacles in the way: the language barrier, different cultural patterns, and so forth: problems of communication. When we do not understand something, our mind starts to project an explanation according to our understanding. This mechanism of projection is found operating within all of us; we have to remove it so that we can come to understand each other. We work toward this goal by elaborating and discussing the different concepts and behaviors that distinguish the different cultures and religions of the world.

The third ideal of our Fellowship is creative living, or constructive self-development. We believe that every human individual is essentially a child of immortality, as is stated emphatically in the Upanishads. God dwells in the heart of every human being, and we all have a vast spiritual potential that lies dormant within us. Through the practice of meditation and following different spiritual principles we have to learn how to develop our latent potentialities to the fullest.

Now I would like to speak briefly about the vision of the man who started the Fellowship. Today we are celebrating the twenty-fifth birthday of the Fellowship. It is certainly a joyous and proud occasion for us. But along with happiness is a deep sadness in our hearts. As we observe the occasion, our minds turn also to the person who founded the Fellowship. His sudden and untimely death is a tremendous loss for all of us. But he left behind a vast wealth of knowledge, his vision of the future, his inspiration and encouragement—all of which we may benefit from.

He had this vision when he graduated from high school and entered college: a vision of the future of humanity based upon integration of the highest cultural values of East and West. He believed that the days of sectarianism are coming to an end. Our need today is the unification of the human race on a spiritual foundation that brings together in harmonious fusion the messages of the foremost spiritual leaders of the race and the spiritual heritages of the two hemispheres of the globe. This ideal inspired him and he was prompted inwardly to prepare himself to serve it. When he came to this country— to San Francisco—he felt that he had to do his life's work here.

Now for us too there are certain happenings which are developing, but we do not see them today, half-concealed behind the surface. These happenings are preparing the ground for manifestation of the new light and power of truth consciousness. How can we ready ourselves to receive them? The practice of meditation and yoga can establish that profound silence in the depth of our beings, so that when the new light shows we are ready to receive it.

The three basic ideals of the Fellowship are: the concepts of universal religion, cultural harmony, and creative or constructive self-development.

In Scotland is told a story about a gardener named John. His minister passed that garden one day, saw John at work, and said, "You have a nice garden here, John!" John answered, "Yes, I have done this, and I have done that, and I have made this lovely garden." The minister responded: "No, no, John, be careful; not you, but you and God, you and God." "Yes" says John," but you should have seen it when God had it to itself." So, this is the gardening of humankind: it is God's work, but God needs cooperation and hard work from us to prepare the soil, make it fertile and receptive, so that when the light of truth is manifested, we are ready to receive it.

The Next Twenty-five Years

As during the first twenty-five years, the second twenty-five years of the Fellowship were filled with diverse activities; here we can only sample them under the categories:

- Lectures
- The Fellowship and California Institute of Integral Studies
- Continuing Scholarship and Publications
- Cultural Activities and Training
- Fine Arts at the Fellowship
- Homemaking Projects for the Membership
- "Lillian's Garden"
- David and Goliath Revisited

Lectures

The Sunday morning talks have remained the centerpiece of Fellowship activities; but with Dr. Chaudhuri no longer present to provide his customary long-term continuity, Mrs. Chaudhuri devised a new format that interspersed lecture series by distinguished scholars with talks by other well-known academicians and cultural and spiritual leaders. Thus the world's religious and cultural traditions have continued to find voice through authorities close to their own communities.

Through recent decades important series of talks have been given at the Fellowship by visiting scholars of Indian thought such as Ajit Mookerjee, Aurobind Basu, M.P. Pandit, Amiya Chakravarti, and Madhusadan Reddy. Resident in the Bay Area for longer periods of time, James Plaugher, Vasant Joshi, and the late V.S. Naravane have come back several times to expound religious, philosophical, and cultural topics through sequences of Sunday addresses. James Plaugher, scholar of Bengal and its heritage, has brought forward the importance of the nondualist tradition and the timeless relevance of Sanskrit studies. Dr. Joshi, academician of literature and religions, has spoken often on the world's rich cultural traditions. And Dr. V.S. Naravane, distinguished scholar in both India and the United States, gave linked talks that covered much of the world's heritage of mythology, philosophy, and literature.

Perhaps two hundred other distinguished speakers have appeared at the Fellowship during recent decades, and it is impossible to begin to list all of them. Among those who typify the rich offerings to the membership and the public are Brian Swimme, holistic cosmologist, speaking on the unfolding universe and humanity's evolving place in the cosmos; Karabi Sen, scholar in both India and the United States, discussing the role of women in the contemporary world, and the unfolding significance of technology in our times; Gobind Bihari Lal, distinguished science writer, presenting a major address on "The Last Century of Hinduism" (December 16, 1979); Dionne Marx Somers, graduate of California Institute of Integral Studies and authority on futurist studies; Dom. Bede Griffiths, who spoke on "Divine Mystery in World Religions" (September 28, 1991); and The Rev. Josephine Cole, who has marked observances of Dr. Martin Luther King's birthday and important Christian holidays, over the years.

Speakers from the Sufi, Bahai, and Islamic traditions have also been included; however, we must end with the observation that the Fellowship has also provided, year after year, an important forum for students, graduates, and faculty members of the California Institute of Asian (now Integral) Studies to present their ongoing research into the world's religions and other cultural activities.

The California Institute of Integral Studies was granted full accreditation by the national system of higher education in 1980.

The Fellowship
and
California Institute of Integral Studies

As requested by the Western Association of Schools and Colleges (WASC), the California Institute of Asian Studies was formally separated from its founding organization, the Cultural Integration Fellowship, in 1974. As part of the advance to full accreditation the Association made a further stipulation for a change in name of the school, and it became the California Institute of Integral Studies before it was granted full accreditation by the national system of higher education in 1980. Thus the subsequent history of the Institute becomes subject matter for another history, to be written at another time.

However, the school has had the goodwill and more tangible supports of the Fellowship throughout the later decades, and several significant contributions of later years need to be recorded here to round out the picture:

37

- Mrs. Chaudhuri continued as vice-president of the Institute until her retirement from the position in the early 1990s. There she continued to embody for successive classes of students the holistic founding vision and the warm interpersonal relationships of the school's early days. She also provided crucial expertise in personnel, alumni affairs, community relations, and maintaining ties with key international scholars and organizations.

- Fellowship member Paul Herman continued to develop and direct the Integral Counseling Psychology programs, and their financial success, together with research grants from the Kern Foundation that he secured and held for several years, contributed vitally to the Institute's cash-flow through several difficult periods.

- Fellowship members Lillian Foote, Jane Taylor, and Helen Desai provided long and distinguished service as members of the Institute's board of directors.

- Other Fellowship members provided volunteer services to the school in a variety of roles; here Lillian Foote, Bobbie Giardot, and Archana Chakrabarti deserve mention as representing a larger corps of volunteers that served the Institute.

- Long after the formal separation of the organizations, the larger rooms at the Fellowship building provided the Institute with space for large meetings, large classes, and graduations that could not be housed in the school on Dolores Street.

• One final contribution must be noted. Shortly after Dr. Chaudhuri's death, the Fellowship established the Haridas Chaudhuri student scholarship, to be awarded each year to an outstanding student at the California Institute of Integral Studies "whose work demonstrates an understanding of the integral philosophy of Dr. Chaudhuri and the intention to creatively extend its spirit into new areas of thought and practice." The awards have helped a number of exceptional young scholars to attain their educational goals.

Continuing Scholarship and Publications

During the later 1970s Dionne Marx Somers became coordinator of the Haridas Chaudhuri publications project and worked energetically with other persons to transcribe and make available for public distribution a number of tapes of Dr. Chaudhuri's Sunday talks. She also completed for publication several unfinished manuscripts, placing a few as articles, and editing others into posthumously published volumes of Dr. Chaudhuri's work:

The Evolution of Integral Consciousness. 1977.
Dionne Marx Somers, ed. Wheaton, IL: Quest
Books/Theosophical Publishing House.

"The Meaning of Karma in Integral Philosophy."
1981. In *Karma: the Universal Law of Harmony,*
Virginia Hanson & Rosemarie Stewart, eds.
Wheaton, IL: Quest Books/Theosophical
Publishing House.

Sri Aurobindo, *Pathmandir,* #8. 1949. In *Karma:
the Universal Law of Harmony,* Virginia Hanson
& Rosemarie Stewart, eds. Wheaton, IL: Quest

Books/Theosophical Publishing House.

The Philosophy of Love. 1987. New York:
Routledge & Kegan Paul.

The Essence of Spiritual Philosophy. 1990.
Wellingborough, Northamptonshire, U.K.:
Aquarian Press.

Cultural Activities and Trainings

As another means of allowing cultures to speak
for themselves, sharing their traditions and wisdom
with others, the Fellowship has regularly honored
the holy days of important religions, and the birthdays of revered spiritual and cultural leaders from
around the world. Thus the birthday of Sri Aurobindo has been marked each year by a special Sunday talk, with a noted speaker drawn from the
American academic/spiritual community or abroad.
This is sometimes combined with a musical event or
relevant seminar held during the following afternoon. The same format has been used frequently
when the Fellowship has observed Martin Luther
King day, Gandhi's birthday, The Mother's birthday,
The Buddha's birthday, or anniversaries of Rabindranath Tagore. Celebrations and memorials for Dr.
Chaudhuri, Uday Sengupta, Vina Armstrong,
Dionne Marx Somers, and other past members and
benefactors also have been held periodically and
have provided additional ways to deepen the spiritual and cultural life of the community.

To convey and preserve a sample of the quality
of these events, I will describe three of them briefly

• June 24, 1984: A special double observance in
honor of Dr. Chaudhuri's birth date, and the ninety-

ninth birthday of Rudolph Schaffer. Rina Sircar, a distinguished teacher of Buddhism both nationwide and internationally, opened the meeting with homage to the two men, followed by a special meditation service. Then Uday Sengupta, distinguished architect and a classical Bharata Natya dancer, performed devotional dances. Rudolph Schaffer discussed his long career as artist and art educator in the Bay Area. And the afternoon concluded with performance on the tabla by Aushim Chaudhuri.

The Fellowship provided avenues for intercultural learning and experience for several decades before much effort along that line emerged in the wider American society.

- October 6, 1985: A celebration of Gandhi's birthday, which began with talks on "The Spiritual Hinduism of Mahatma Gandhi" and "Gandhi and Nonviolence." Following luncheon the Fellowship building was filled with three hours of traditional Indian Mela activities: folk dancing, garland making, demonstrations of Bengali floor decoration, and spinning in the handloom manner.

- June 18, 1995: "Remembering Haridas Chaudhuri," with a video presentation of his life, in place of a Sunday lecture, followed by luncheon, and shared memories from participants in it who were in attendance.

41

- On March 25, 2000, as the first fundraising event toward the Fellowship's fiftieth birthday celebrations, Helen Desai presented a "History and Art of the Sari," an afternoon as visually rich as it was informative.

Of course major Christian holidays are honored along with those of other traditions. The annual evening Christmas party was organized for many years by Lillian Foote, who as part of it led the group in singing songs and carols, and herself provided a memorable recitation of "The Night before Christmas."

As from the early years of the Fellowship, there have been continuing classes in meditation, yoga, tai-chi, Indian classical dance, ethnic dance of various peoples, and Chinese brush painting.

The Fine Arts at the Fellowship

The fine arts have been very well represented among Fellowship activities, beginning with San Francisco artist and decorator Vina Armstrong as an early member of the board of directors, to the present with art-scholar Helen Desai on the board. There have been many concerts by artists from India and elsewhere abroad, as well as recitals and concerts by local artists and groups. For example, during one two-month period, October-November 1994, Nanda Banerjee sang Classical Indian songs at the Fellowship; Sri Karunamayee brought songs from the Sri Aurobindo Ashram to the Fellowship; and a larger gathering at St. John's Presbyterian Church in Berkeley listened to Aushim Chaudhuri, Zakir Hussain, and The Rhythm Experience in a fundraiser for the remodeling of the Fellowship's home on Fulton Street.

Dance performances have been part of many events, as well as full programs themselves. Again, artists from around the world have danced at the Fellowship, but perhaps those dances that remain strongest in memory as perfectly coordinated in every detail were given on special occasions by member Uday Sengupta. Uday Sengupta was also a very talented painter in the classic Indian forms. He presented to the Fellowship a number of striking works; the Durga panels used in the Durga Puja festival are the largest. Following the death of the artist, board member Don Boysen donated a larger collection of artworks by Uday Sengupta, which Raj and Helen Desai have been very helpful in conserving.

Poetry, too, has played its part through the years at the Fellowship as a vehicle of multicultural learning and creative self-fulfillment. Joseph Kent and Sally Love Saunders have provided ongoing energy to the group of poets that has usually shared one or more annual poetry events with the membership.

Homemaking Projects for the Membership

In recent years, as the building and gardens on Fulton Street have aged, the Fellowship has devoted considerable resources and efforts to update them for comfort and safety. After the earthquake of the late 1980s, the building was retrofitted to conform to latest standards, and at the same it was made accessible to disabled persons. The organization also took this opportunity to redesign and modernize the social rooms downstairs, providing additional space for meetings and events apart from the principal room used for Sunday lectures. At her passing, Lyne Duchamp left a bequest that has been used to restore the painted decorations in the entrance lobby; and most recently a new library has been completed to house the Fellowship's expanding library. Consequently, on its fiftieth anniversary observances, the Fellowship had a handsomely restored home for the celebration. Beginning early in 2000, Mrs. Chaudhuri initiated planning for those events through several large and small committees, and as the year went along increased energy went into the efforts. To assist her, the board of directors appointed Professor James Ryan, a scholar of Hinduism and Eastern studies, to serve as assistant director of the Fellowship.

"Lillian's Garden"

Early in 2000 Mrs. Chaudhuri also sparked the membership's enthusiasm to celebrate the ninety-eighth birthday of Lillian Foote with suitable warmth and flair. It is notable that although a group of persons were involved in the planning, and nearly a hundred members came to the party, the secret was kept so well that when Mrs. Foote appeared at the Fellowship for a "brief stop" on April 1, 2000, she was genuinely surprised to be met inside by the sound of "Happy Birthday" being sung by her large group of friends, who stayed most of the afternoon to share good wishes, visit, and enjoy a Fellowship luncheon that characteristically included dishes prepared according to several cultural traditions.

The climax of the event was the dedication of an area of the Fellowship grounds dubbed as "Lillian's Garden." The garden, outfitted with a fountain, arbor, benches, and a table, is newly planted with vines, shrubs, and colorful lilies and spring flowers. Marked by a plaque that preserves its name, the lovely vital garden seems a symbol both of Mrs. Foote's progress toward her centennial, and the

44

Fellowship's vigorous approach to its second fifty-years.

David and Goliath Revisited

During a half-century that has seen the rise of great multinational corporations and the inroads made into traditional cultures worldwide by materialistic North European-American enterprises, the Cultural Integration Fellowship—with its few hundred members and its credo of intercultural growth and harmony, universal spiritual values, and creative self-fulfillment—may seem a small, quiet-voiced David confronting a huge bronze-armored Philistine. Surely the greater weight of physical and popular resources is available to Goliath, in both the Biblical story and present-day experience.

Yet in its first fifty years the Fellowship has not relied upon physical and popular resources so much as upon strength and guidance from the "Guru within" and "five smooth stones from the brook." Such orientation, and astute use of tools that lie at hand, have allowed the Fellowship to contribute to its members and to society in proportions far greater than its available resources would have indicated. It has fostered deep inward changes in many persons. It has provided avenues for intercultural learning and experience for several decades before much effort along that line emerged in the wider American society. In Dr. Chaudhuri's books it has produced scholarship that speaks to the cutting-edge issues of the twenty-first century. It has founded, launched, and then set free a graduate school, perhaps the first and most distinguished of its kind in the world, a school that continues to make exciting advances into the new millennium. And it has illustrated, amidst a culture that sometimes seems obsessed with values of individualism, that fellowship and interpersonal concern are tools of great potency, too.

With five such "stones in its wallet" the Fellowship has advanced through its first fifty years. If it continues to employ its sling during the next half-century, who knows what more may be accomplished?

Vern Haddick is Emeritus Professor of Integral Counseling Psychology at California Institute of Integral Studies in San Francisco. He edited *Transcendence and Transformation: Writings from California Institute of Integral Studies,* New York: University Press, 1983. Vern has been a member of the Fellowship since 1971.

A Spiritual Life Unfolding

by Haridas Chaudhuri

1.

The atmosphere in India has a spiritual *charge,* as it were. When I was a little boy, for example, five years old, my grandmother would tell me stories, as grandmothers all over the world do. But frequently she would tell me stories about spiritual things. For instance, once she told me a story about a powerful king. He was marching triumphantly through all parts of his country with hundreds of soldiers and courtiers. Cities turned out to honor him. But when marching through an obscure part of his kingdom, all his horses and men suddenly came to a total, unexpected stop. And where was it? At the humble cottage of a sage, a *rishi,* who was deep in meditation.

It was all very impressive to me that the mighty king with all his soldiers and horses was stopped. What power could the sage have? He was, apparently, doing nothing, just sitting there in meditation, but he had tremendous power. This impressed me. "What is this power?" I asked myself. The profound impression of meditation and spiritual power which my grandmother conveyed remained with me all through the years, at the back of my mind. And then, at about age ten, I had a very small personal experience which was also inwardly important. We were playing outside. Nobody had a watch on, and someone wanted to know the exact time. I suddenly said what time it was. They went to check inside the house, and it was exactly the time I had said. So I was surprised. How could I do that? I began to notice that when there was a special "state of the mind" I could do certain things. But when that state was not there, I could not. Gradually, I realized how much of life depends on one's *inner consciousness.*

These little incidents reinforced my interest in meditation. I began to think, "Well, if so much depends on the condition of consciousness, then inducing the right condition is of paramount importance in my life." It is important because in that condition one can function so much better.

I became very interested, therefore, in finding techniques for inducing the proper consciousness. Then once, when I was studying descriptions of different meditation techniques and reading about the experience of oneness with Being, with the ground of all existence, suddenly I *became* it. With my whole being I responded to it. All the different pieces of experience fit together into a whole, a very meaningful whole.

This state of consciousness continued for some time. Then gradually, problems began to develop. This experience produced alienation from the outside world—I found myself sometimes very absent-minded. The family would give me some chore to do, but I was so absent-minded that I didn't do it properly, and this caused me some embarrassment from time to time. I was, to use that amusingly accurate phrase, living in a different world. I also began to feel an alienation from what we may call the instinctual self, my physical existence. My whole life schedule—study, meditation, and so on—had become constellated around the new experience of Being I had had. But then I found there was not too much room, in that earnest schedule of mine, for enjoying life. And that, I did not like.

In 1924, when I was a high school student, I began to have some spiritual aspiration. Near my school in Calcutta was the Ramakrishna Vedanta Center. I used to read their books and talk with some of the members. One day, when I was reading a particular book—Swami Vivekananda's *Jnana Yoga*, which means "yoga of knowledge" the knowledge-approach to self-realization—I was deeply moved, and for a few days I was in a different kind of world. It was a peak experience along the line of the knowledge tradition in India. It lasted in a very intense form for three or four days, and then at a lower level for a few days after that. It changed my life: the spiritual ideal came to the forefront of my consciousness and I began to reorganize my whole life on this new basis. There was a feeling of great joy, of oneness with Being—"Brahman" as we call it. And there was a resulting feeling of alienation from the ordinary, material world.

In the beginning it was not painful; that would come later. In the beginning it was a feeling of bliss, and it began to influence me to structure my life. You see, when I began reading *Jnana Yoga* I took it very existentially. I was looking for guidelines for life.

It had been a "big bang" experience! It was fine, it was very exciting, that I had an experience of the kind Vivekananda talked about. That made me feel good. But then I began to feel bad, because of the growing awareness of my alienation from my instinctual, physical existence. Because I have, along with my strong spiritual interest, a strong vital nature, a passionate nature. I have the will-to-enjoy, you see. So I said to myself back then, "This doesn't seem to be very good—why should one deprive me of the other? Why not have both?" I wanted to enjoy this world, and I wanted to enjoy the spiritual world. That is how it should be!

Then a friend gave me a small book from the library, Sri Aurobindo's *The Mother*. I read it and it was another important experience. I felt in touch with a great mind. His was a novel approach, and he became right then and there my guru, my personal teacher. He lived in a very far-away part of India but I decided to seize the first opportunity to visit him and in the meantime prepare myself by reading more of his books.

Aurobindo said renunciation, asceticism and self-suppression do not lead to total fulfillment in life. I became very enthusiastic about his views and took them to heart, because they seemed to fit in with my own interests. I was interested in everything from body-building and enjoying life, to knowing truth and Ultimate Meaning. I did not want to exclude any part or aspect of life.

My reaction against renunciation was so strong, however, that as the years passed and I went on to college I lost faith in religion and spirituality altogether. What was meaningful to me was the humanistic, rational approach—participation in life and the development of whatever potential and possibilities one may have: physical, vital, mental. Religion and mysticism seemed like very dreamy stuff—insubstantial. It was quite a change. Still, of course, at the back of my mind, was the thought that there might be something to it, the urge to know truth, the ultimate meaning of life, but first I had to explore what was uppermost in my mind.

Maybe later on, I thought, I will have a second look at these other things.

Many authentic spiritual leaders have gone through a period of skepticism and negation. I think this is good. Someone who does not go through a period of doubt cannot wholeheartedly realize God in the true sense of the word. Without going through this period of interrogation and challenging, realization is founded on naïve faith. I don't think unquestioning acceptance has much substance.

One sees, for example, certain people becoming excited about meditation or Zen or whatever, without exercising their critical faculties at all. They go overboard into emotionalism and total dogmatic acceptance. One can see that their belief and practice is not the result of their own inner convictions. It is rather an escape, a flight from the reality of their own lives. There's nothing much one can do about it, because if you bring in a critical note they'll think that you don't know anything. I find it best in these cases to wait until they feel the need for guidance, and then to seize the opportunity to help them with their questioning.

I believe, of course, in the growth process, and I might add, the *individual* growth process. In the spiritual heritage of India it is very much emphasized that there is *no set pattern of growth, no standardized path,* which all are supposed to, or should follow. The main Indian tradition in such matters takes into full account the different psychological types to which people belong—the character structure or psychic makeup of different individuals. There are four or five main psychological types which are considered, and four or five main paths.

In Indian psychological thinking the total human psyche has, broadly speaking, five interrelated aspects or dimensions or levels of consciousness.

These are, first, the physical level, the body; then the instinctual, vital, energetic aspect; then the aesthetic, emotional, perceptual; then the intellectual or rational, including such higher mental functions as abstract thinking, philosophical thinking, up to the gnostic vision of the universe as a whole. These are different gradations of the rational-intellectual activity of the psyche. And then, finally, comes the highly intuitive, the purely spiritual, transcendental aspect. Within these levels, *sub*-gradations are also distinguished.

> *I am a Purna Yogi, which means Integral Yogi, which is an integration of karma (action), Jnana (knowledge), and bhakti (love).*

Naturally, all these different functions or aspects of the psyche are interrelated and interpenetrating—one cannot completely separate them. When we make a classification, we do not mean that they are watertight compartments that are mutually exclusive. But roughly corresponding to these five aspects, we can speak of specific ways to self-realization. In the Indian tradition there is, for example, the approach of knowledge (Jnana Yoga), the approach of action (Karma Yoga), the approach of love (Bhakti Yoga) and the approach of self-analysis (Raja Yoga). There are many traditional approaches that each person can use singly or in combination, according to his or her psychological type. In terms of the psychological types, I am a karma and jnana combination. My beginning was jnana and karma came later. As for my approach, I am a Purna Yogi, which means Integral Yogi, which is an integration of karma (action), Jnana (knowledge) and bhakti (love).

I entered college in that frame of mind: rational, critical thinking was all-important and spirituality seemed to be an escape from the problems of the world. But through all my vicissitudes, I had felt an inner guidance, a vague and yet definite awareness of my future, a sense of purpose, of what was to be done. There was not much wavering in that. For example, in my college days I had a feeling that I would come to the West, and I studied those subjects which would be useful for this purpose: for example, traditional Western philosophy and also the Western philosophers of the day—Whitehead, Russell, Bradley, Gentile, and so forth.

2.

After graduation, the desire which had been suppressed so long—going to see Aurobindo in far-away Pondicherry—returned. I wrote to Aurobindo, telling him how I had long been interested in his philosophy. At the same time I mentioned that I had no faith in religion or mysticism. "I don't believe in that. I believe in two things. One is free, independent, critical thinking—thinking things through. The other thing is self-discipline and creativity."

He wrote back, inviting me to come to Pondicherry. So, in 1937, I took the train, accompanied by another philosophy professor and his wife. When the train arrived in Pondicherry they were both very happy: they told me how fortunate it was that we were just in time to participate in the evening meditation at the ashram. I was not interested in meditation and did not understand their excitement. However, I decided to go along with them.

During the meditation I watched everything very carefully, the atmosphere there, the attitudes of the different people who came to meditate. The first thing that much impressed me was the massive silence. There were about two hundred people there. But there was silence, silence reigning supreme in the whole place. No one uttered a word. They came and sat in perfect silence, and then, Aurobindo's spiritual co-worker, the Mother, as she was called, came and conducted the meditation.

The first three days there, I was all eyes: I met different people, trying to find out what they were doing, why they were there, what they had received. I saw some papers written by Sri Aurobindo in answer to their questions or problems. So for the first three days, I did research. I got more knowledge about meditation. When as a schoolboy I had first practiced meditation, I did not have much knowledge about it. So I practiced it mechanically, and soon gave it up. But now because of this new information about the technique and the core of meditation, on the fourth evening I thought, "Well, what's the harm? I always believe in adventure, exploring new paths without closing the mind to anything. Maybe it is time to give a second try to meditation and see what may happen." So on that fourth evening I made a sincere attempt, and it was very good!

It was my first good experience in meditation and it was important to me. I became interested in meditation again. Now I understood for the first time what true meditation meant. People were surprised to see that from that time on I was the first to come to the meditation place, and the last to leave. Naturally after you have that glimpse, you want to consolidate it. I became interested in it with my total being. Gradually, meditation allowed me to reach towards the transcendental dimension of life, the realm of profound ineffable things, the pure spiritual dimension.

We start our lives as children with a kind of immediate participation in the world, doing things according to social mores and our likes and dislikes, in general conformity to society. But gradually our likes and dislikes emerge more and there comes a kind of negation or rebellion. We are supposed to conform to some social standard or law and we rebel against it. We feel a clash between our personal selves and all this authority. Then later on, hopefully, we mature and reconcile both on a high level: our need for social laws and our awareness of their limitations. We integrate them into our life without seeing them as the final standpoint. This is the socializing state of development.

In the life of spiritual seekers there is also this *dialectical rhythm*. It goes through affirmation to negation, thesis to antithesis, and then that which was rejected comes back in a new form. From the spiritual standpoint, the dialectic process *includes* the socializing state of development. After this stage, the triad of spiritual thesis-antithesis-synthesis begins: a great moment comes and one becomes thoroughly disenchanted with this whole *samsara* (the flux of empirical existence, the external reality of the world with its social and ethical laws and rules). The whole thing loses its significance. It is all samsara, a big game, without ultimate truth in it. This is the moment of alienation, of disenchantment with all this world. Before you were part of it, adjusted to it, did not like much of it but wanted some of it, and so on. Then, suddenly, one day the whole world looks like a farce, a circus. With all your being you are hungry and thirsty for some deeper reality. This is the existential crisis. It is the same kind of thing that Arjuna experienced on the battlefield of life in the *Bhagavad-Gita*. Then comes the true renunciation. Like the Indian prince who became Buddha, this is the time when the person "leaves his kingdom," goes in search of truth, disenchanted with the whole world as a whole.

Many times, after my experience at Pondicherry, I would enter the state of alienation. I would have a strong urge, for example to give up my professorship, leave everything and move to Pondicherry. But every time I entertained that idea, I heard another, deeper voice within me saying, "No, both have to be integrated." It became clear that this was the better way—that the thesis of the world and the antithesis of its renunciation had to be synthesized.

But it was difficult. At times I would become so submerged in duties and professional responsibilities that I would long to give up everything. I had no time for the things I enjoyed, like meditation, study, and so on. I had to do unpleasant things I didn't like, spending boring days going through examination papers. I would become fed up—why waste so much time? Then, I would remember Sri Aurobindo saying that the principle of *karma yoga*, the way of action, acknowledges that there are many unpleasant things in life. I would recall that in karma yoga one must accept the unpleasant with the pleasant, the boring with the exciting. This unpleasantness is only a habitual, accustomed response. If one has the right attitude and orientation, then that which appears unpleasant can become pleasant. There can be a *transformation* which takes place with the change of your attitude.

So long as our mind is as it is, it always sees the dualities: pleasant-unpleasant, exciting-boring, sublime-vulgar. Sometimes these polarities become truly oppressive. But they are only relative to our attitude at a particular stage of evolution. Later these polarities are transcended, and we have the experience of divine joy. We see the inner essence of a thing, whatever it is, and it give us joy. *Where there is the right inner attitude, physical, external renunciation is not necessary.* This is the truth which I have found written unambiguously in the different scriptures, and if it is so then we need to act accordingly. Whatever I am now seeing to be unpleasant, boring, not good, or undivine is a relative thing. And that relativity can be conquered by change of consciousness.

> *Whatever you do, however small and insignificant it is, you do it in the spirit of self-offering to the Divine . . . even your smallest action is sanctified by the divine touch.*

For example, at one time I was appointed examiner of the university, which meant that I had to read a thousand examination papers: just imagine! It was so boring, so much wasted time! Then I caught myself, "Well, this is relative to my way of looking at it." One of the basic principles of karma yoga is that whatever you do, however small and insignificant it is, you do it in the spirit of self-offering to the Divine. You do it as an instrument of the Supreme Being. Then you are attuning yourself to divine consciousness, and even your smallest action is sanctified by the divine touch. So I said to myself: "For me grading papers is boring, but for the student whose paper I am reading now it is very important. It will mean so much to him, the mark I give him, and if I am careless in the matter because I am bored, he will suffer. I will do my best and by rendering a real service to him, I am also serving God."

We always have to weigh the pros and cons and make a decision about whether such tasks are suppressive or repressive or enforce a "top dog" attitude. For example, when I accepted this kind of task I made up my mind that I would never spend the whole day just doing this. There were certain fundamentals in my life which I would not sacrifice. Time for meditation, for example: I would not sacrifice that. I had an order of priorities. When it came to the point that I had to sacrifice all, then I would not go that far. I would say, well, every day I will do fifteen papers, and accordingly, I would make a schedule. There has to be sufficient joy and happiness in life; then we can accept some amount of unpleasantness alongside of it, and hopefully transform it. And we have the additional satisfaction of doing something for the sake of others. There is a service orientation: in serving the human, you're serving God. It's a way of offering to the Divine through the serving of God *in* human beings. And seen *as a part of the whole*, it's fine, it becomes a part of yoga.

3.

The first aspect of Integral Yoga is taking into account the unique nature of the specific individual makeup. I am completely against giving advice or trying to help without taking into account the unique fullness of the individual. There are various traditional approaches, as I have mentioned. An individual can choose any of these approaches, and the only essential thing is that at the start the goal be clear. Where is the process going? What is the direction, and what is the purpose? With a clear understanding of goals, a person can begin anywhere with whatever rings a bell.

The second aspect of the Integral path is one's organic relationship to society or to the human family—the human aspect. When I say this I'm fully aware of what I'm rejecting, because many spiritual systems think of the individual as a spiritual atom, a self-sufficient entity which can have spiritual fulfillment outside society. I don't believe this! I believe that the organic relationship to society is an essential ingredient of the structure of a person's being. A person is mutilated, to a certain extent, by completely withdrawing from society, and the spiritual fulfillment will not be complete. Aurobindo very much believed this and practiced it. During the Second World War, he was highly criticized for making public statements in favor of the Allies and giving a very handsome donation to the Allied War Fund. People said, "What business have you as a yogi to interfere with politics?" But for Aurobindo, politics and yoga were *one.* This was at a time when Hitler was going from victory to victory, and people thought the Axis powers were going to win. But Aurobindo said: "To my inner vision, the power behind Hitler and Mussolini is already crushed. It is a question of time until that is manifest, and there is no doubt in my mind that the Allied forces will win. And that will be good," he said, "because in spite of all their limitations, the Allies are walking in the direction of evolution." So, this is the second aspect of Integral Yoga, being organically related to society, to humanity, to human evolution.

The final aspect is existential restructuring: every individual has unique potentials and unique limitations. These will be developed as part of the self-actualization of the individual. We each have a unique contribution to make to society and the world if we wish, if we can actualize our potential.

It is transcendental consciousness which gives you real rootedness in the *ground* of all existence, which brings you spiritual liberation. It is this consciousness which gives your organic relationship to humanity, to human evolution and to the cosmic process as a whole. Here we each play an active role, making our own little contribution, participating.

Self actualization is not the end. It must be supplemented by humanistic participation in evolution. And in back of it all is full freedom. I mean full freedom from all forms of attachment. It is transcendental realization which brings the light of full freedom to an individual, allowing absolute *fearlessness* in life and self-expression.

> *Self actualization is not the end. It must be supplemented by humanistic participation in evolution. And in back of it all is full freedom from all forms of attachment.*

There is a creative power in the spirit of higher consciousness which is capable of actually *transforming* this apparent "burden" of body and world into a perfect image of the Divine. And when that transformation takes place, instead of appearing as a prison-house, or a burden, the body and the world become temples of the inner divinity. Aurobindo calls this creative and transforming power the *Super-mind.* He considers it as one of several levels of higher consciousness. Some of these levels broaden your perspective and worldview but do not have a true transforming power. Aurobindo says that the Supermind is that level which not only broadens your mental horizons but also has the ability to actually transform inconscient physical existence. He saw this transformation as the next step in evolution. We are still in the transition period of this step, but there are indications from all sides that we are approaching the next stage. There is, for example, a new awakening towards higher values, towards more inclusive consciousness. There is a growing realization that these are very important for effective and lasting solutions to the basic problems of humanity, that they are of paramount importance to transform our inner being. Change of the externals of life, such as the economic structure of society or of political arrangements, making international pacts, or restructuring the judicial system, these are fine—they are needed steps in the right direction. But changes in the externals of life are not enough, because in the last analysis, it is people who will operate even the best political-social machine. The person behind the machine is of fundamental importance. However, ideally we may change the structure of society, as long as the inner person does not change, we will not solve our basic problems. What is needed is to change our inner being toward a wholly integrated consciousness—the resolution and harmonization of all our inner dichotomies and polarities.

In Integral Yoga there is a hierarchical scheme of life where knowledge occupies a lofty position, but it is *not* ultimate. After knowledge must come the translation of your inner vision into your life. If you don't do anything with it, then it is not real *samadhi*. I don't like calling things ultimate; everything is unfinished business, still evolving. I think our human spirit is a continuous process—ever-widening horizons with increasing fruitful self-expression. Selecting a particular condition as "ultimate" makes a person dogmatic. It is a blind alley. It's a very luminous alley, but a blind one. Transpersonal experiences for example, have great value, but I do object to the ultimatistic thinking that is often used when people speak about them. Various people speak and write of *ultimate* positions, experiences, ideas, endpoints, needs, drives, and a tendency to "ultimate states of being". Ultimatistic thinking is another version of absolutist thinking. It creates dichotomy, which creates dogmatism. The concept of "higher" I do go along with, but not "ultimate." Because however high one goes, there's still beyond.

After knowledge must come the translation of your inner vision into your life.

This ultimatistic thinking is based on a *static* view of samadhi. Aurobindo says that when you enter samadhi you begin a new journey. All that nonsense about enlightenment as a one-time flash, and then it's all okay! Not at all. It is *the beginning of a new life*, a life of enlightenment. And it is a new *process*.

62

Aurobindo says that when the groping for the light of truth ends and you enter into the light, then you begin your real journey. Plato also says that it is a process of progressively seeing into the immeasurable vastness of the truth. He doesn't say that you just see it and that's all.

Let me give a concrete illustration. Gandhi was right in the forefront of power politics and different parties would come to him. He would say, "Let's not hurry to a decision." He would go into silence and meditate. Then he would come out and say, "I have seen the inner light—here is my decision." But having made the decision, he would still keep an open mind: he would never dogmatize and say, "This is the absolute truth I have received in meditation, the Voice of God." It was for him a dynamic interplay between intuition and critical thinking. There was a wonderful synthesis here of humility and open-mindedness, and at the same time he followed his decision, because at the given moment it was the best that he knew.

As soon as you equate a condition of consciousness with the absolute, you are massacring the absolute. Every state, or condition, is a state or condition. It is part of the flux of time. It cannot be absolute. *All experiences are partial manifestations of the absolute.* The absolute is the all-embracing totality. The absolute isn't even evolution: It *includes* evolution. When you choose something for an absolute, you set up an absolute division. "That is the absolute; all this is false." Then all your other experiences—your human relations, washing dishes, eating food—become unclear to you, can indeed begin to seem meaningless. This happens whenever we equate an aspect of reality with the absolute. Many people who have perfectionist strivings fall into a similar absolutist trap. When we strive for perfection, we are thinking that absolute perfection is something that can be attained. In the process, we can accumulate a lot of nervous tension which results in psychological damage. No state of existence is perfect or ultimate. The human being is a process. All human life is a process.

There is a very good principle which can help us to steer clear of the ultimatistic trap. This is the practice of *nonattachment.* Many people here in America, as soon as they have a nice experience, become attached to it, and then make strenuous efforts to recapture that delightful experience which never comes again. It becomes a very pitiable condition. As we meditate, for example, different experiences will come, and we observe them, we learn from them, but we must not let ourselves become attached to them. When they come, we understand, we are absorbed—when they go, we let go. Such nonattachment gives you dynamic freedom. It leaves you poised in your own self. Being firmly entrenched in your own being, you refuse to be carried off by alluring experiences. This is the principle.

All experiences are partial

manifestations of the absolute.

The important thing from the Integral standpoint is not "What experience? What power?" but "What are you going to do with it? How are you going to use it?" Therefore operate from the center of your being, from which you can judiciously use the power that comes and the experiences that come.

Enlightenment means not only expansion of consciousness, broadening of horizons, but also deep inner value-consciousness. No matter how much power a person may have, one may still be a devil's disciple if value-consciousness has not been purified. This is the essence of spiritual realization: value-consciousness. Otherwise there is always the danger of exploiting power for self-aggrandizement. The ideal guru is one who helps the individual realize his own *inner* guru. Now unfortunately, many people have become guru-worshippers, devoting themselves entirely to the outer guru. So I tell them, "You must remember, the real goal is not guru-realization. It is *self*-realization."

Editor's note: This article is adapted from "The Meeting of East and West: A Conversation with Haridas Chaudhuri," *Synthesis*, vols. 1-2, 1975. That interview was conducted by Betsie Carter-Haar and Stuart Miller; Mr. Miller has kindly consented to this reprinting.

Basic Principles of Integral Living

by Haridas Chaudhuri

Integral yoga defines the spiritual destiny of life as dynamic and complete self-integration. It is important to realize the inmost essence of one's own being as a unique center of creative self-expression of Being.

There are three essential ingredients in the realization of complete self-integration: psychic integration, cosmic integration, and existential integration.

Psychic Integration

Psychic integration implies a harmonizing of the different aspects of personality. There are some conflicting elements of human nature. Instinctual drives, impulses, and urges are inherent in the unconscious psyche. In opposition to many of them is the rational will of the conscious mind. The conscious rational will is molded by the social and cultural forces of the community to which an individual belongs.

The unconscious psyche is the source of limitless energy. It is the powerhouse of the individual. Besides the sexual impulse it includes the vital impetus to grow and develop. It includes the holistic impulse, the drive to attain ever-widening wholeness of being, as well as the self-assertive will to power. It is the habitat of repressed wishes and desires as well as original creative urges. The unconscious is indeed the region where the vulgar and the sublime, the demon and the angel, dwell side by side. It is where light is hidden in darkness, and darkness is capable of turning into light.

The unconscious psyche carries in its deepest layer memories of the protracted evolution of the human race. Crucial experiences of evolving mankind are deposited therein as archetypal images. The symbol of God as the cosmic father or the cosmic mother is operative as a dynamic force. Symbols of the eternal child, the eternal feminine, and the old man are part of the inheritance of the unconscious. Symbols of the serpent as irrational impulse and of the bird as the high-soaring intellect also belong to the structure of the unconscious.

The rational consciousness is shaped by socio-cultural forces. It acquires the ideas of good and evil, of god and devil, of heaven and hell, from the cultural environment. It learns the art of self-discipline with a view to applying its psychic energy to the fulfillment of socially approved goals. It is persuaded to suppress certain promptings of the unconscious on the strength of socially recommended standards of excellence and perfection. Thus a conflict between the conscious and the unconscious; between impulse and law, is set up in various forms in the heart of the individual. When this inner conflict and tension is more than the individual can handle, all manner of emotional disturbances appear.

Various extremist and one-sided attempts are often made to resolve the inner psychic tension. Some persons prefer the spontaneity of passing impulse to the restraint of reason. They decide to follow indiscriminately the promptings of inward urges. They are guided by the pleasure principle or the hedonistic concept of "Eat, drink and be merry." But unfortunately hedonism breaks down by its inherent paradox. It proves cruelly self-defeating. The consciously pursued pleasure is ever elusive, like a will-o'-the-wisp. Our keenest pleasures are those which come unexpectedly or as the by-product of our selfless devotion to some objective value. Moreover, when divergent desires begin to conflict with one another, there is no way to reconcile them in accordance with the pleasure principle. The result is a life of chaotic impulses pulling in different directions, or a life of aimless drifting on the flow of vanishing pleasures.

Some persons again prefer perfection to pleasure. They swing to the opposite pole from hedonism. They tread the rigorous path of austerity and self-immolation. They are activated by unflinching devotion to some standard of perfection held forth by society. In doing so they ruthlessly suppress the inner promptings of their own unconscious mind. They allow the superego to become oppressive and tyrannical. A pervasive sense of human sinfulness corrodes their soul. The soaring flames of Puritanism burn up their vital fluid like scorching rays of the sun. In consequence, they are likely to develop behavioral oddities and eccentricities, if not more serious psychic disturbances. They have to pay indeed a heavy price for failure to come to terms with the unconscious.

Some persons again may prefer an independent quest of the spirit to socially prescribed perfection. They choose the ascetic path of exclusive devotion to pure transcendence. They decide to advance alone towards the Alone. In doing so, they do not hesitate to suppress the social and humanitarian side of life. They may even develop an uncompromising attitude of hostility to society. The follies and foibles of social life, its superficiality and conventionality, may drive them to extreme antagonism and withdrawal. But in suppressing the social side, they have also to suppress some fundamental urges of the psyche. Because, in the last analysis, psyche and society are inseparable. Their all-out search for the spirit in disregard of social demands and psychic urges, may, however, by virtue of single-minded devotion, produce some spiritual gains. Through intensification of inward consciousness they may gain unusual aesthetic insights or mystical visions. Such spiritual gains undoubtedly bring some satisfaction to the soul. But they represent only a partial achievement. The denial of the social and instinctual aspects of life means considerable self-mutilation. In scaling the heights of the spirit, one is uprooted from the depths of the psyche. One attains brilliance at the cost of wholeness. In rising up to heaven; one loses contact with mother earth. There may be a meteoric rise to prominence, but the opportunity for balanced growth and integral self-fulfillment is lost.

Psychic integration implies the harmonious growth of personality. In the interest of balanced growth, one has to come to terms with the fundamental instinctual urges of one's nature. One has to pay attention to the distinctive bent and inclination of the individual psyche. In an attempt to reconcile impulse and reason—the unconscious id and the conscious ego—one discovers a deeper principle of unity in existence. It is the principle of the higher self. It does not allow the lopsided development of mind at the cost of body, or of brawn at the cost of brains. It does not encourage the one-sided growth of intellect at the cost of emotion, or of sentimentalism at the sacrifice of calm judgment. It does not permit the tyrannical growth of social consciousness at the sacrifice of psychic needs or the rebellious spirit of whimsical and arbitrary behavior such as is subversive of the social order.

Since psyche and society are essentially inseparable, one has to take into account the demands of society even for the sake of psychic growth. One has to realize that however imperfect the norms of social morality may be, one cannot reject one's fundamental relationship to society without self-mutilation. Even when one resorts to the remotest nook of solitude one carries society with oneself, because society is part of the soul. The soul has the vital need to love others and to be loved by others. Its very essence lies in relating itself to fellow beings. So, in getting away from the sphere of social relation and action, one smothers the social ingredient of the soul. One may criticize society and try to remold it, but one cannot entirely ignore society or discard it. To renounce society permanently for its imperfections is like rejecting one's wife for her illness. Likewise, to suppress the unconscious psyche for its dark impulses is like throwing away the baby with the bath water. For the light is hidden right in the heart of darkness.

Cosmic Integration

The foregoing discussion of the need for psychic integration leads by a sort of inner dialectic to the concept of cosmic integration. The psyche cannot be fully integrated without realization of its relationship to nature and society, i.e., to the cosmos. Psyche and cosmos are inseparable aspects of one

70

concrete reality. The fundamental reality is neither the psyche nor the cosmos but the psyche-cosmos continuum. It is neither the isolated self nor the independent universe, but the self-in-the-universe or the universe-for-the-self. It is atman-brahman (thou-that or I-that).

In point of truth there is no self-enclosed entity in the universe. Relations are vital to existence. To exist is to be related. An atom exists so far as it is related to a field of energy. A plant lives so far as it is related to a physical environment of air, light, water, and soil. An animal lives and moves so far as it is related in various ways to its own species and other species. A human individual grows so far as it responds in various ways to nature, to society, and to the stirring of the eternal within himself.

In order to achieve health, happiness, and wholeness in psychic growth, one has to maintain integral relationship to the total environment including nature and society. To shut nature out from one's life is to injure oneself. That is why the artificial modes of living in many modern societies are so detrimenttal to health and vitality. Fresh contacts with nature are always revitalizing. Fresh air, fresh water, sunshine, open space, silent communion with the sublime in nature—such things are essential for the blossoming of the human psyche. Exposure to the beauty and grandeur of nature is a source of profound inspiration to the soul. That is why places like the Himalayan regions, the Grand Canyon, and Niagara Falls have been the home of spiritual rebirth for thousands of sensitive souls.

Harmony with nature also implies a feeling of kinship with the animal kingdom. By mercilessly killing animals, one kills the spirit within oneself. By being heartless to the mute sufferings of one's world mates, one smothers the finer sensibilities of one's own nature. By setting oneself in violent opposition to the rest of creation, one creates division and discord within one's own being. Such division and discord enfeeble and disfigure the personality. We cannot achieve psychic wholeness by inflicting wounds upon the wholeness of life. A feeling of oneness with the realm of nature, a sense of life's sacredness, a reverence for all life, is indeed vital for the holistic growth of human personality.

To shut nature out from one's life is to injure oneself.

The psyche also blossoms in the medium of social action. The more a human gives the self in the spirit of love and friendship, the more he or she experiences the delight of self-expansion. The more one becomes vitally concerned with the welfare of fellow beings, the more one enlarges one's own being. An active interest in others is an essential means to the bursting of the ego-shell.

An individual takes the first step beyond egocentricity in learning to subordinate personal pleasure and comfort to the interest of the family. Or, perhaps the first lesson comes from one discovery of a real "chum" from among one's circle of acquaintance. When one is ready to surrender personal likes and dislikes for the satisfaction of a chosen friend, one may even be ready to die for the friend's sake.

In the course of further development the welfare of the community to which one belongs may become a distinct motive of action for the individual. Next, the welfare of one's country or nation may become a dominant spring of action. For the sake of the nation one is ready to sacrifice personal and family interests—perhaps even to sacrifice one's life.

In the course of still further development an individual may become actively concerned with the welfare of the international human family. From "My country, right or wrong" s/he now advances to the motto: "Humanity before my country." One feels convinced that human welfare is indivisible. The best interest of one's country is indissolubly bound up with the welfare of the world community. Or, the conviction perhaps grows within that the ultimate good of country is entwined with the concept of truth and justice, with the notion of God. Taking a long-range view, the policy of aggressive nationalism or militant expansionism is bound to react adversely upon the ultimate good of one's own nation. The different peoples of the world do indeed exist by being closely related to one another. They are essentially interdependent. They are inseparably associated members of the cosmic whole. They live, move, and have their being in one indivisible cosmic medium. An active realization of this truth produces cosmic integration.

Existential Integration

But neither psychic integration nor cosmic integration can attain the fullness of actuality without the discovery of the eternal spirit, of which both psyche and cosmos are different modes of manifesttation.

However much a person may be rationally convinced of the need for psychic harmony, the discord between different elements of personality such as passion and reason, instinct and intellect, emotion and understanding, threaten to be irreconcilable. One achieves a measure of compromise, but the final resolution of psychic conflicts may appear impossible on the psychic level. The secret of complete psychic harmony lies in the realization of the eternal man—of the timeless dimension of existence. It is there that the ultimate unity of the psyche is to be found. That is why the full integration of the psyche can be accomplished only in the light of existential experience, i.e., a direct insight into the ultimate ground of existence which is timeless. An existential contact with the nontemporal abyss of Being is indeed essential for the consummation of psychic integration.

The same is also true of cosmic integration. However much one may be rationally convinced of the need for social and cosmic harmony, there seems to be a fundamental and irreconcilable discrepancy between self and society, between psyche and cosmos. It appears impossible to dissolve such discrepancy by the persuasiveness of reason. One can at best hope to achieve a certain measure compromise between individual growth and collective good. But the secret of complete cosmic harmony lies in the realization of the timeless root of the cosmic flow—of the eternal dynamically present in evolution and history. The ultimate unity of psyche and cosmos lies hidden in the timeless depth of Being. It is only an existential plunge into the abyss of Being that can reveal the principle of social harmony. It is in the light of supra-cosmic realization that the integration of psyche and cosmos can be carried to perfection.

Thus we see that the final step in integral self-development is existential integration, i.e., integration with the ultimate ground of existence, which is timeless. The discords of time can be turned into elements of harmony only in the context of the eternal. The process of self-adjustment to the psyche and the cosmos can be consummated only through contact with the eternal.

But we should hasten to observe here that even the eternal is not to be equated with the fullness of Being. The eternal is no doubt the most fundamental dimension of existence. But it cannot certainly be said to be the only dimension of existence. Being in its fullness is multidimensional. The eternal represents the element of pure transcendence in Being. It represents the mystic's unfathomable mystery, the yogi's imperturbable peace and self-poise. But Being is also manifested in time in the form of evolution and history. It has the aspects of growth, development, and creative self-expression which are inseparable from life. The historical is no less essential to the structure of reality than the nontemporal.

Mysticism is right in emphasizing the value of the eternal. But mysticism makes an error in equating the eternal with the whole of Being. Such a false equation has dominated much of traditional religious thinking. It has given rise to religious pessimism, negativism, and other-worldliness. The mystic's false equation is the opposite of secularism's error in equating time with the whole of Being. The latter has given rise to Epicureanism, materialism, and nihilism. The truth is that Being is the unity of time and eternity, of evolution and transcendence. It is the unity of nature and spirit, and of the historical and the nontemporal. An integral understanding of the multidimensional Being is essential for the balanced growth of personality. In order to attain the wholeness of being, an individual has to be true to the kindred points of heaven and home, of eternity and time.

Principles of Creative Existence

Now, how to achieve existential integration? And how to organize one's life in such a way that existential experience may function as the basis of harmonious and fruitful living? In other words, what are the fundamental principles of creative existence?

There are four fundamental principles of creative existence: aspiration, action, meditation, and love.

There are four fundamental principles of creative existence: aspiration, action, meditation, and love. The spiritual unfoldment of persons involves a twofold choice or commitment. It begins with a definite decision to discover the ultimate ground of existence, i.e., to realize God. It ends with a final decision to make a supreme sacrifice of oneself for the sake of the Divine dynamically present in the world, i.e., for the sake of cosmic welfare.

Aspiration

Aspiration is the initial decision involved in spiritual life. It is an all-out search for the eternal. It is a sincere and determined resolve to organize one's

76

whole life on the basis of spiritual values. It is the indomitable will to find out the meaning of God in the context of one's own personal experience. Theistic arguments on the one hand and agnostic reasoning on the other are alike meaningless in the absence of concrete personal existential experience. If any actual person in history did ever have a direct glimpse of the Divine, others also must be capable of having the same in some measure. When an individual feels ready to undertake the task of gaining such a direct insight, whatever the cost involved, one has the authentic aspiration. The extent of the willingness to stake one's whole life on it is the measure of aspiration.

There is an important distinction between aspiration and ambition. Ambition is the longing of one's immediate desire-nature. It is hankering after wealth and affluence, power and position, name and fame. But authentic aspiration is the stirring of the spirit, the divine spark. While ambition is a movement of the ego, aspiration is a reaching out of the soul beyond the boundaries of the ego. It is the awakening of the super-personal factor in human personality. It is the response of our inner being to the call of the eternal or to the impact of the evolutionary world-process. Aspiration is a calm and steady flame, in which egocentric cravings and desires are more and more consumed. Ambition is the self-assertion of the individual as an individual. Aspiration is the self-affirmation of the individual as an active center of the universal. Aspiration evolves out of ambition at a crucial moment of inward growth. It is the transmutation of ambition by the power of self-transcendence inherent in human beings.

We have already observed that aspiration represents a decision to realize the eternal and to live for the eternal. Strictly speaking, such a decision is not made, it evolves. It happens to the individual in the course of the inner growth of consciousness. It takes place in the depths of the soul, in the luminous dark of the unconscious psyche, before it appears in the mind as a conscious decision. When it emerges as the central purpose of life, a vast amount of psychic energy is released. The individual can now function with the combined resources of the whole personality.

Authentic aspiration is known in religion as the unqualified love of God. When the flame of such love is kindled in the soul, the whole being is set on fire. It produces an expansion of consciousness to the dimensions of the universe. Selfless action is the spontaneous outcome of such self-expansion.

Action

So, we come now to the notion of action as the second fundamental principle of creative existence and integral growth. As we have already seen, action is of the essence of human reality. It is not only a means of attaining freedom, but also the essential content of that freedom. It is the spontaneous outpouring of freedom.

There is no such thing as absolute inaction. Even when one is sitting very idly, the mind becomes busy riding high on the crest of thought-waves, perhaps vigorously day-dreaming. When one goes to sleep, the conscious mind is put to rest, but the unconscious psyche gets busy projecting and fulfilling in subtle form some of its buried impulses and desires. In rejecting the world of action and going to the hills, one carries the world within the mind and expresses a negative reaction to the world in various ways in the medium of contemplation. Through contemplation, one acts upon the world from the realm of fantasy and ideas. Actions also suppress psychic impulses and emotions which are positively oriented to the world of action. And, of course, physiological processes inside the organism are all the time going on without interruption, during wakefulness or sleep, activity or idleness, in society or out of society.

The most important question then about action is this: How can we make our actions more and more meaningful? How can we relate action to the cosmic purpose of existence, to the ultimate goal of evolution? How can we bring action into harmony with the full freedom of the spirit?

There are certain forms of action which hinder spiritual unfoldment. They inflict damage upon the free growth of personality. They alienate us from our spiritual roots and occasion gradual self-dissipation. They may deaden the soul and crush the spirit.

For instance, when action is reduced to a dull monotony, to a humdrum routine affair, it becomes an imprisonment for the human soul. Society has a responsibility to see to it that the sphere of social action does not degenerate into a dehumanizing prison-house. The same thing happens when action becomes too mechanized. When there is no room for free choice of initiative, action becomes like a dead burden for the soul. It is the spiritual duty for those who enjoy freedom, power, and enlightenment, to refashion the social structure in such a way that action assumes the form of meaningful and joyful self-expression.

As an essential ingredient of Integral Yoga, the principle of action has three aspects: *self-expression, self-poise,* and *self-donation.*

We each have a primary task of concentrating on the development of our latent possibilities. Our course of training and education must be determined accordingly. If our inner psyche points in the direction of a future as an engineer or doctor, it is outrageous if we are compelled for any reason to become a businessman or a priest. If our inner psyche holds forth the image of a poet or painter, it is foolish to become a politician or tycoon. When we are allowed to grow according to our own unique law of becoming *(svadharma),* we can rise to the height of our possibility, and our action becomes meaningful and joyful.

This does not mean that a successful engineer must invest all his or her time and energy in the field of engineering. Or that an ideal politician must devote all time and energy exclusively to political action. Oftener than not, there are many other interests and urges in a person besides one central ideal. For instance, a politician may have a great deal of interest in gardening, in music, in writing poetry, in playing golf, etc. In that case it is a challenge to find time to fulfill some of these interests in a way that is consistent with the major work and responsibility as a politician. Suppression of strong psychic urges is definitely harmful to the growth of personality. A basic principle of Integral Yoga lies in lending an attentive ear to the inner promptings of one's own psyche. A person who discovers this inner light and counts it as a major factor in the decision of affairs finds action immensely fruitful and gratifying.

Another principle of action is self-poise. One may feel sure about the actions one should perform. One may also have a measure of control over one's own actions, but can never tell beforehand how far one will succeed in the endeavor. It is difficult to know how others will react, or whether society will appreciate these actions. One may find that those very people whose welfare one intends to promote misunderstand and even deny one. One may find out that there is no necessary connection between honest and meritorious work on the one hand and social recognition and reward on the other. So an attitude of non-attachment to consequences is very much needed to sustain one's works of social service. When in a given situation one decides after mature deliberation that a particular course of action is good for all concerned, proceed to do it regardless of consequences.

> *Nonattachment to consequences produces serene self-poise.*

In an attempt to translate one's crucial decisions into action one has to go ahead fearlessly, setting aside considerations of profit and loss, praise and blame. Such disregard of, or nonattachment to, consequences produces serene self-poise. It enables one to maintain inward calmness and even temper in the midst of all changes of fortune. One acts, and yet does not act. There is a core of imperturbable immobility to all movement. It is non-action in action. One plays one's part to the best of one's ability and leaves all consequences in the hands of Providence. One has no control over consequences anyway. Virtue has its gaze fixed upon cosmic welfare. Its ear is attuned to the call of destiny. It is sheer expediency to allow the consideration of immediate consequences an upper hand. Expediency seeks reward in outward circumstances. But virtue is its own reward. It is the joy of creative self-expression. It is the joy of self-giving to the universal.

That brings us to the third principle of action, namely, the principle of self-donation. From the spiritual point of view, the ultimate motive of action is the spirit of self-donation to cosmic welfare. It is one's dedication to the inward vision of the meaning of life and evolution. It is one's active concern with new values emerging in one's consciousness. It enables one to stand entirely on one's own. Opposition and antagonism cannot coerce one into submission. Allurement or blandishments cannot cajole one into standard conformity. One's ultimate loyalty is to an inward vision of the truth. One stands alone, armed with the invincible strength of a relationship to the eternal. But precisely by virtue of taking a stand all alone, one offers oneself without any condition or reserve at the altar of the ultimate good of humanity. Self-donation may not be in conformity with the established authority and tradition. As a consequence, it is not conditional upon social recognition and reward. One gives oneself by an act of supreme sacrifice to the unborn future of humanity. Unforeseeable new values emerge out of such unconditional self-giving.

Meditation

The courage to act alone regardless of consequences is born of the awareness of a relationship to the eternal—of one's absolute relationship to the absolute. Meditation is the channel through which one discovers this relationship.

In the practice of Integral Yoga, meditation and action are inseparable. Meditation, which is the art of intensifying inward consciousness, has various methods. Some of these methods are discussed in detail in the last two chapters of *Integral Yoga*. Here the fundamental principles of meditation as an element of the integral approach may be briefly indicated.

There are five basic principles of integral meditation: dynamic self-offering, psychic exploration, self-energizing, critical evaluation, and existential experience. In the practice of Integral Yoga, dynamic self-offering to the cosmic reality is of paramount importance. It provides the right starting point and sets the proper mental framework. The spirit of self-offering is the real beginning of integral meditation, whereas the perfection of self-offering is its ultimate goal. Of course, an individual may start with any other method of prayer or meditation particularly suited to one religious or cultural background. But if one is interested in integral self-development, one has to come round sooner or later to the concept of self-offering.

The attitude of dynamic self-offering to the cosmic reality adequately reflects the concrete human situation. The human individual is not an isolated, abstract, self-subsistent entity. One does not exist apart from the cosmic whole. One is nothing apart from one environment, natural and social. Individuality becomes meaningful only in the context of the evolutionary advance of the dynamic world-spirit. So, the method of introspection or detached self-observation, carried to the end, may prove misleading. It may easily produce extreme introversion. It often encourages the introverted to wish for static and isolated self-abiding *(kaivalya)*, which may be peaceful but not productive. Isolated self-abiding is liberation negatively conceived as emancipation from the evolutionary movement of life. It is the static spiritual ideal. Enamored of the

83

timeless dimension of the self, it fails to appreciate the significance of the historicity of the self. The human is essentially an historical being. One cannot completely fulfill oneself without actively relating to the march of history. Withdrawal from the historical order is a form of self-mutilation. Moreover, the static ideal is rooted in a false conception of the self as immobile and isolated consciousness. In actual reality, the self is nothing apart from its relationship to the cosmic whole. And as a unit or member of the cosmic whole, the self is not immobile but tremendously dynamic.

The method of passive self-offering to the divine or the eternal may also prove misleading. When a person is absolutely passive in submission to the divine, one may frequently be carried off one's feet by waves of emotion or dark suggestion welling up from the depths of the unconscious. When there is total passivity or a vacuum, one can never be sure how that vacuum is going to be filled. Undivine forces often masquerade in the name of God. The need for a sharp discrimination between the divine and the undivine—between what is conducive to, and what is subversive of, cosmic welfare—never can be dispensed with. Consequently, self-offering to the Divine must be accompanied by constant vigilance and discrimination so that the forces of ignorance may not allure and mislead.

The attitude of passive self-offering to the divine has often stimulated the image of blissful self-absorption in the absolute. Many mystics in the past were lured by this image. They rightly rejected the theory of the self as isolated and self-subsistent consciousness. But they could not entirely shake off the influence of the static spiritual ideal. They retained the notion of the self as immobile and detached consciousness. Only, in their view, the individual was nothing apart from the absolute. So, it was through the annihilation of individuality in the absolute that consciousness was to be realized in its passive purity.

> *There are five basic principles of integral meditation: dynamic self-offering, psychic exploration, self-energizing, critical evaluation and existential experience.*

The ideal of blissful self-absorption in the absolute was based upon the inadequate conception of the individual self as a product of ignorance *(avidya)*. According to integral philosophy, the individual self is emphatically not a product of ignorance. It is not on illusory appearance of the absolute. Nor is it a passive medium of the universal. The self is essentially a free creative center of the universal. It is therefore through dynamic self-offering to the cosmic reality that the self can hope to realize fully its inmost essence. It is through active participation in the historical order that the self can function as a significant member of the cosmic whole.

The basic reality of life cannot be defined in terms of the universal alone. Nor can it be defined in terms of the individual self alone. It can be expressed only in some such terms as the self-as-related-to-the-universal. Self-cosmos is the indivisible unit of existence. Hence integral meditation can truly begin only with the focusing of attention upon the dynamic relationship in which the self stands related to the cosmic reality.

In practicing meditation, one relaxes, lets go of mind and body, and calmly reflects upon one's ontological status as an active center of the Divine. One offers oneself, heart and soul, to the cosmic creative principle, to the universal life force, so that one's ultimate purpose of life may be revealed. Meditation is an act of dedication to the cosmic purpose of existence. During the course of meditation, whatever thoughts, impulses, desires, feelings, or memories may arise in the mind, one has to observe them with patient analysis and sympathetic understanding and offer them to the Divine, so that they can all be coherently organized around the central purpose of life.

The next important phase of meditation is self-exploration. As one gets into the mood of relaxed self-observation and self-offering to the Divine, the unconscious mind is more and more activated. One begins to probe into the depths of one's personality. Different levels of the unconscious are revealed. Repressed wishes and long-forgotten memories suddenly come to the front. Unsuspected potentialities are brought to attention. Hidden powers of the mind disclose themselves. And thus self-exploration brings about a process of self-energizing.

Self-energizing reaches its height when the divine spark leaps into a flame. Science tells us that a vast amount of energy is hidden in the positive nucleus of the atom and that it can be released. Similarly, there is a vast reservoir of energy hidden in the depths of the unconscious psyche. Some have called it the power of God slumbering within us. Some have called it "the coiled power" (kundalini)—the central psycho-physical power lying dormant in human personality. In the course of psychic exploration this central energy potential is eventually activated. That marks a turning-point in self-development. It touches off a kind of psychic explosion, a conversion of consciousness, an undreamt-of intensification of existence. A free flow of limitless energy is set in motion. The process of meditation now becomes effortless and spontaneous. Life re-captures its original freshness. One feels the presence of a much deeper power within oneself. It appears irrepressible and all-engulfing. The supreme spiritual task now lies in channeling this boundless energy along right lines.

> *The supreme spiritual task now lies in channeling this boundless energy along right lines.*

In dealing with power there is always a great need for careful evaluation and intelligent control. Someone driving an automobile at high speed must make sure that the brakes are in good order and that one is capable of applying them at the right time. People who are in charge of atomic energy know what a tremendous responsibility it is. Various precautioary measures have to be adopted to prevent its falling into irresponsible hands or slipping into monstrous abuse. Likewise, the awakening of the fundamental energy potential in the human is a psychic breakthrough which has its brilliant promise and also its dismal danger. Unless used judiciously with proper control it may burn itself up too rapidly. Even though it may shine for a while with uncommon brightness, the dazzling glare may be short-lived. One cannot afford to trifle with high-voltage power. Even the spiritual longing has to be duly restrained. The presence of power calls for patience and calm judgment. A mature sense of responsibility is needed. A clear sense of values must provide direction to the vital impulse.

Meditation is not an exercise in occultism. Without an insight into the higher values of life, occult power may prove destructive to self and society alike. That is why critical evaluation is an essential ingredient of meditation. The more a person is sincere in self-offering to the cosmic reality, the more the sense of values is sharpened. The more a person is purified in heart with a flaming dedication to the supreme, the more one is lifted above the corrupting influence of powers. But after the ground has been prepared with purity of the heart and clarity of the vision of truth, power assumes the form of divine grace. It enables one to make giant strides towards the fulfillment of one's destiny.

The final phase of meditation is existential experience. It means some kind of direct insight into the ultimate ground of existence. In Buddhism this insight has been called *bodhi* or *prajna*. Zen calls it *satori*. In Hindu philosophy it is called *samadhi*. It involves a sense of rootedness in the eternal and a feeling of oneness with the universal. There is an immediate experience of the oneness of all existence. All the multitudinous forms of being, the innumerable living creatures, the divergent peoples, races and nations of the world, are experienced as unified in one ultimate ground. The apprehension of the ultimate has been called unitive or cosmic consciousness by Christian mystics. All the great religions of the world, especially foremost mystics in world religions, point to the unitive cosmic consciousness as the crowning fulfillment of spiritual effort.

From the psychological point of view, existential experience signifies the awareness of a hitherto obscure and veiled new dimension of existence—the dimension of the nontemporal. The non-temporal is the abode of transcendence and freedom. When a person makes an existential contact with the nontemporal, one has an exciting sense of liberation from all bonds. In respect of one's nontemporal mode of existence one rises above the sphere of cause and effect, breaking the fetters of the law of karma and enters upon a new phase of life—the life of participation in the timeless consciousness. The freedom and spontaneity which were lost in outgrowing childhood are now recaptured on a higher plane.

The child's spontaneity is based upon untutored impulse and unknowing innocence. It is an unstable equilibrium. The development of reason and conscience is sure to disturb it. As the child is introduced to the sociocultural dualities of good and evil, god and devil, heaven and hell, and so on, the freshness and spontaneity are gone. One experiences some kind of fall from paradise. Along with strife and struggle, a life of taboos and inhibitions begins. But the holistic growth of personality may eventually result in discovery of the non-temporal dimension of being. Upon such discovery freedom and spontaneity reappear on a stable basis. Paradise is regained on a deeper level of personality. Neither the temptation of devil nor the wrath of God can destroy it any more. The conflicting noises of life's power politics are hushed into silence in the sanctuary of the timeless.

Love or *Lila*

Broadly speaking, there are two levels of awareness of the nontemporal. First, the nontemporal is experienced as abstract transcendence. The pulse and the heartbeat of the world process are not felt there. The music of the spheres has no responsible chord there. The ebb and flow of the tide of cosmic evolution is not registered there. Naturally therefore on one level of ontological insight one says "No" to the world. The drama of life fades into unreality. The discords of evolution dissolve like a bad dream. The mystic denial reaches its highest point.

In Hindu philosophy such participation has been called Lila, i.e., joyful cooperation with the dynamic world-spirit (Krishna).

But on a deeper level of awareness of the nontemporal, the mystic denial itself is denied in a higher affirmation. The nontemporal is now perceived to enfold within itself the profoundest secret of the world process. The evolutionary movement of life and history reappears clothed in a new significance. It is realized that if the world is nothing apart from God, God is nothing apart from the world. God is the unity of the world. The world is the diversified expression of God. The dichotomy of God and world is dissolved in the nonduality of the nontemporal. The perspective of the nondual, nontemporal lends a profound meaning to the dynamic presence of God-in-the-world. The affirmative awareness of the nontemporal may be called *integral existential experience.* It is the apprehension of the ground of existence as the indefinable unity of God and the world. Such integral experience is the basis of illumined creative living. It is the basis of love as selfless participation in the creative advance of cosmic evolution. In Hindu philosophy such participation has been called *Lila,* i.e., joyful cooperation with the dynamic world-spirit *(Krsna).* This is the significance of Sri Krsna's exhortation to Arjuna in the *Bhagavad-Gita.* Krsna advises Arjuna to be inwardly united with the Divine and outwardly act on the battlefield of life. Arjuna is to act in a spirit of fellowship with the Divine. The objective of such action is to carry to fruition the purpose of human evolution. It is to establish the kingdom of truth, justice and progress. But since it is the purpose of evolution itself, the best way to serve it is to abandon selfish motives and personal attachments. Purest action is that which is free from any tension of inner conflict or any compulsion of emotional attachment.

Lila is cosmic love. It is the crowning glory of Integral Yoga. It is not static union with the eternal. It is not the peace of self-annihilation in the absolute. It is not the ecstasy of life and world negation. Nor is it a mode of ego-fulfillment. The pure flame of cosmic love leaps into being only through the burning of the ego. There are some who shy away from immediate contact with the eternal in order to preserve their personal wishes and predilections, their attachments and emotional bonds. They are eager to participate in life with their egocentric individuality kept intact. They are unwilling to relinquish their inherited and ingrained notions of good and evil, god and devil. This may be called ethical love. It shows active interest in social amelioration. But it is afraid of rising above social morality in favor of a direct encounter with the eternal. The naked touch of the eternal is devastating to the fixed notions of conventional morality and dogmatic theology. It effectuates a radical transvaluation of values. It crucifies egocentric individuality with all its pet desires and flattering creeds.

For Integral Yoga, cosmic love is the secret of self-perfection. It is dynamic love of the Divine actively engaged in the world process. It is non-attached love of the world as visible manifestation of the Divine. It is participation in the being of the world with a self-poise in the heart of nonbeing. A person who contacts the eternal no longer has any sense of external compulsion or socially imposed obligation. When one acts for the good of humanity, one acts with a sense of fun, freedom, and the joy of spontaneity. Having had a glimpse of the ultimate meaning of life, one cannot turn away into the peace of private seclusion and stoic indifference. One feels the luminous urge within to fulfill one's role in the cosmic drama to the best of one's ability in a spirit of supreme dedication to cosmic welfare.

This article is a slightly revised version of the fifth chapter ("Basic Principles of Integral Yoga") from Haridas Chaudhuri's book, *Integral Yoga: the Concept of Harmonious and Creative Living.*

Overview of the Integral Yoga

by David Hutchinson

Note: This article preserves a talk given by David Hutchinson at the Cultural Integration Fellowship on April 29, 2001.

Opening Remarks:

I want to thank Bina Chaudhuri for coming up with the idea of this series of talks, and for her long-standing and tireless work. Without her, this Fellowship would not exist. Bina exemplifies what her husband Haridas wrote in his book, Mastering the Problems of Living, about the integrated person: "creative harmony and balance—a dynamic interplay of the inner and the outer" (Chaudhuri 1968, 34-35).

This yoga is based upon the experiences of Sri Aurobindo and the Mother over many decades, experiences that started in the early years of the century and continued to the Mother's death in 1973. The complete collection of their talks and writings comprises about 60 volumes, so a single talk like this is necessarily sketchy.

A succinct statement of the yoga was stated by Sri Aurobindo in a letter in 1934. It begins:

The teaching of Sri Aurobindo starts from that of the ancient sages of India that behind the appearances of the universe there is the Reality of a Being and Consciousness, a Self of all things, one and eternal. All beings are united in that One Self and Spirit but divided by a certain separativity of consciousness, an ignorance of their true Self and Reality in the mind, life and body. It is possible by a certain psychological discipline to remove this veil of separative consciousness and become aware of the true Self, the Divinity within us and all. (Aurobindo 1974, 26:95-97)

Distinguishing Integral Yoga from other spiritual paths is not easy, because the distinction can be subtle. All spirituality aims at finding the core of existence, God, the divine consciousness. Yet there are significant differences between this yoga and Patanjali's raja yoga, the yoga of the tantras, Kundalini yoga, Vedantic philosophy, or Indian religion in general.

This yoga aims at a contact with the Divine that ultimately encompasses all of our being that uses every possible point of contact. The Mother says "Essentially, you must be able to find this oneness with the Divine in all forms, all aspects, in every way that has been used to reach Him. And you must go beyond that and find a new way . . . It does not depend on the forms you have chosen: necessarily, you will have to pass through in order to find what is behind. But if you want to transform your nature and your being, and if you want to participate in the creation of a new world, then...one must include everything and contain everything in one's consciousness" (The Mother, 1956, 8:245-246).

In this yoga you will find the traditional and the radical, links to the past and pointers to the future. It builds upon the discoveries of luminaries who came before, but challenges us to come to grips with entirely new possibilities. One defining characteristic of this yoga is its insistence on transformation. Transformation means a change of our current existence, a reshaping of everything that we are—the mind, the emotions, even the physical body—into a likeness of divinity.

One defining characteristic of this yoga is its insistence on transformation.

It is possible to have transcendent and even absolute spiritual experiences, to achieve unity with one's soul or with God or liberation from the world, and not undergo this transformation of our external nature. Sri Aurobindo writes "It is only some yogas that aim at a transformation of any kind" (Sri Aurobindo 1974, *Letters,* 22:11). Most yoga aims at liberation, *moksha,* or union with God. Because this yoga looks to convert everything about the human into the divine, it is called complete (*purna*), or Integral. And this very completeness makes it complex, multifaceted, slow paced, and less amenable to simple definitions.

How to go about transforming oneself into the nature of the divine? What should we do? The first step is to get in touch with that Divine consciousness; this is the beginning point for all of us, to contact that reality. In terms of transformation, Sri

Aurobindo and the Mother discovered a critical truth: that higher consciousness has a power, what is called in Indian religion the Divine Mother, or Shakti that can effect this transformation. This higher consciousness can work more completely, more directly, with better results, than we do when acting from our current awareness. Sometimes it is spoken of as the power of the soul over its nature. "This power of the soul over its nature is of the utmost importance in the Yoga of self-perfection; if it did not exist, we could never get, by conscious endeavor and aspiration, out of the fixed groove of our present imperfect human being; if any greater perfection were intended, we should have to wait for Nature to effect" (Aurobindo 1974, *Synthesis*, 21:602).

However, we are not born with access to this higher or divine consciousness; we must turn towards it, make an effort to find it. This is our first responsibility: to make that link, get in touch directly, in practical awareness, with the divine. The final chapter of *The Life Divine* makes this point emphatically. Sri Aurobindo says "In the growth into a divine life the Spirit must be our first preoccupation." And, he says, to get at "the secret mainspring, which is the Spirit itself, is of cardinal importance....This then is the first necessity, that the individual, each individual, shall discover the Spirit, the divine reality within him. . . a divine life must be first and foremost an inner life" (Aurobindo 1974, *Life Divine*, 19:1020-1023). Because the Divine is everywhere, any aspect of our subjective inner life or our outer life can be used to make contact, but past teachers have found broad thoroughfares, natural mechanisms in the human being that are conducive for this turning and con- act. Throughout their writings and talks Sri

96

Aurobindo and Mother speak of knowledge, emotion, and will as three main powers of consciousness. Using these to turn toward divinity is the triple path of the *Bhagavad-Gita.*.

In the chapter titled "The Principle of the Integral Yoga," in *The Synthesis of Yoga,* Sri Aurobindo writes "Our synthesis takes man as a spirit in mind much more than a spirit in body and assumes in him the capacity to begin on that level. For that reason our initial stress has fallen upon the utilization of the powers of soul in mind and the turning of the triple key of knowledge, works and love in the locks of the spirit" (Aurobindo 1974, 21: 586).

The initial, indispensable step in this yoga is to develop a real, felt, working contact with the Divine. Once that is available, the central method of the Integral Yoga comes into play: surrender. Surrender is the practice of actively turning towards this "otherness" that you feel within, and allowing it to guide your spiritual life. It may be felt as a presence, as a light, as a force, or in other ways.

In a letter, Sri Aurobindo writes "Surrender is the main power of the yoga, but the surrender is bound to be progressive; a complete surrender is not possible in the beginning, but only a will in the being for that completeness—in fact it takes time; yet it is only when the surrender is complete that the full flood of the *sadhana* is possible. Till then there must be the personal effort with an increasing reality of surrender. One calls in the power of the Divine Shakti and once that begins to come into the being, it at first supports the personal endeavor, then progressively takes up the whole action, although the consent of the *sadhak* continues to be always necessary. As the Force works, it brings in the different processes that are necessary for the sadhak, processes of knowledge, of bhakti, of spiritualized action, of transformation of the nature" (Aurobindo 1974, *Letters,* 22:525).

In the individual, the emergence of this Divine power, this Shakti, takes place progressively; for a long time some degree of personal effort remains necessary. This giving over of oneself and the resultant transformation is not instantaneous or miraculous; it is more like the growth of a child into an adult. The Divine takes up the action itself of sadhana; this progressive switchover of the source of action is the key to the Integral Yoga. Sri Aurobindo writes,

> this is the only [way] I know by which the taking up of sadhana by the Divine becomes a sensible fact before the preparation of the nature is done. In other methods the Divine action may be felt from time to time, but it remains mostly behind the veil till all is ready. In some *sadhanas* the divine action is not recognized: all must be done by *tapasya* [personal effort]. In most there is a mixing of the two: the tapasya finally calling the direct help and intervention. The idea and experience of the Divine doing all belong to the yoga based on surrender. (Aurobindo 1974, *Letters,* 22:588)

This is the secret of the Integral Yoga. Most yoga, in practice, deals primarily with preparation of consciousness through personal effort. In this yoga, the "method" is to contact a higher consciousness, and then let it do what is necessary to change your nature. This is one reason that the Integral Yoga is said to begin where others end: most yoga aims at contact with the Divine; this yoga has that as a preliminary aim, but after making contact begins the stage of transformation. You drill a hole in the dam separating yourself from the Divine, and then step aside as the water comes trickling, then pouring, then gushing through, with its immensely greater force. The "action" that Sri Aurobindo mentions is a real force, real illumination, a felt consciousness, and it has its own method. "The change effects itself through process of nature, not therefore by any capricious magic, but an ordered development and intelligible process...[it] may seem a miracle to the intelligence, but it still proceeds by law of the truth of Spirit" (Aurobindo 1974, *Synthesis*, 21:602). It has been noted by many disciples through the years, and continues to be a cardinal element in *sadhaks* today.

Most yoga aims at contact with the Divine; this yoga has that as a preliminary aim, but after making contact begins the stage of transformation.

Consciousness is a substance, it has grades, powers, textures. "these experiences of the Divine are not mental constructions, not vital movements; they are essential things, not things merely thought but realities, not mentally felt but felt in our very underlying substance and essence" (Aurobindo 1974, *Letters*, 22: 169). Or as he says of one grade of the higher consciousness, "All experience there tends to be concrete, there are no "abstract" truths as in the mind—even thought in the overmind is a concrete force and a palpable substance" (Aurobindo 1974, 23:1162).

In this yoga, inner discovery and change comes first, even though transformation is seen as a goal. Until the higher consciousness becomes a practical reality in one's life, transformation isn't possible. In a talk in 1955, the Mother cautions against imagining one can start at the end. She says:

> The first movement is a withdrawal of consciousness from this total identification with outward and apparent things, and a kind of inward concentration on what one wants to discover, the Truth one wants to discover. Many people who are here forget one thing. They want to begin by the end. . . first of all it is necessary to take the way of interiorisation. (The Mother 1955, 7:354-355)

Successful interiorization leads to a number of well-documented spiritual experiences, such as liberation from the confines of the ego; feeling the silent witness; identification with the universal Self; seeing the Divine in everyone and everything in the world; separation of consciousness in *samadhi;* union with the spark of divinity in the heart. There is no set progression or sequence for these achievements; rather, there is a great variability in the manner they come to each individual. These are important steps or markers in a complete yoga; they belong to the spiritual legacy of humankind, and this yoga gives them their rightful place as essential building blocks for an integrated spiritual life.

Achievements such as these are generally seen as the final goal of spirituality. What could possibly remain to be done after union with God or the soul? Many paths say that if one is identified with God, nothing else matters, there is nothing else to be done. But the goal of the Integral Yoga is a complete transformation, right here, of everything that we are: not just our inner awareness, but our rashes, bumps, and twitches. If identification with God were all that mattered, there would be no reason for an Integral Yoga; methods for achieving union have been known for thousands of years.

We talked about contacting the Divine through going within, and surrendering to that force and consciousness. But what exactly is it that Integral Yogis do? The Integral Yoga stresses principles over particular methods. Yes, Sri Aurobindo and the Mother gave advice on specific and detailed aspects of the lives of their disciples. But they realized that flexibility in the practices one takes up at any time is necessary. Every person has a different set of abilities, problems, and needs. They did not set up a single system of practices for everyone to follow.

If identification with God were all that mattered, there would be no reason for an Integral Yoga.

Nevertheless, two movements or forces of consciousness are central to this yoga: equanimity and aspiration. Equanimity (*samata* in Sanskrit) is the condition for all other achievements in yoga, and it can be developed in each part of ourselves: the mind, the emotions, and the body. The Mother says "Almost the very first step in Yoga demands that you must keep a perfect equanimity in the presence of all beings and things and happenings. Always you must remain calm, untouched and unmoved; the strength of the Yogi lies there" (The Mother 1929, 3:100). Developing equanimity in this yoga is the counterpoint to the eightfold path in Buddhism, or *yama* and niyama in Patanjali's yoga: it prepares one for further realization (Aurobindo 1974, *Letters,* 22:143). Other yoga paths see spiritual evolution as taking place through goodness, *sattva*; this yoga treats equanimity as a power that enables further transformation.

Desire and ego form the central problems in human nature, and conquering them leads naturally to equanimity. Of these problems, Sri Aurobindo writes,

> These are the two knots of our subjection to this ignorant and divided Nature, desire and ego-sense. And of these two desire has its native home in the emotions and sensations and instincts and from there affects thought and volition; ego-sense lives indeed in these movements, but it casts its deep roots also in the thinking mind and its will and it is there that it becomes fully self-conscious. These are the twin obscure powers of the obsessing worldwide Ignorance that we have to enlighten and eliminate. (Aurobindo 1974, *Synthesis,* 20:94)

The triple path of the Gita forms the basis of working with these two problems: "the way of knowledge through the mind's discernment between Reality and the appearance, the heart's way of devotion, love and surrender and the way of works turning the will away from motives of self-interest to the Truth and the service of a greater Reality than the ego" (Aurobindo 1974, *On Himself,* 26:95-97).

Equanimity creates the conditions for surrender to the Divine to work, to be safe and effective. It has a specific purpose. The Mother explains it this way. "If anyone among you has received spiritual forces, forces of the Divine, Ananda, for example, he knows from experience that unless he is in good health he cannot contain them, keep them. He begins to weep and cry, gets restless to expend what he has received. . . . To be well balanced, to be able to absorb what one receives, one must be very quiet, very calm" (The Mother 1953, 5:23). In other words, equanimity of mind and heart opens the door for the higher consciousness to come and to stay.

The second main principle, aspiration, is itself a force of the inmost soul within us. In this yoga the soul is called the psychic. Encouraging and strengthening one's aspiration is a powerful means of contacting the soul and opening to its influence. This force is often likened to the flame, Agni, of the inner divine, and it can be felt as such deep in the heart. In her first talk to a group of disciples in 1929, the Mother describes this flame of aspiration. "Is the Divine the supreme fact of your life," she says, "so much so that it is simply impossible for you to do without it? Do you feel that your very raison d'etre is the Divine and without it there is no meaning in your existence?" (The Mother 1929, 3:1)

Aspiration calls a response; it is like a lighthouse beacon sweeping across the universe, looking for the answering ship of the divine awareness. It is not just an emotion, but can originate in any part of oneself. For example, in 1954, when the Mother was already deep into her yoga of the body, she said "Each part of the being has its own aspiration...There is even a physical aspiration...the cells of the body...with all their strength, all the consciousness they contain, they aspire to this transformation . . . [they] open in this

103

way to receive the Force" (The Mother 1954, 6:391-392). Equanimity prepares the being; aspiration calls the higher consciousness.

The interplay between these two powers of consciousness, equanimity and aspiration, exemplifies a question that arises for all who aspire for another consciousness: the seeming contradiction between effort and non-effort. This yoga sees effort and non-effort falling on a continuum. Effort has its place: until that other awareness can act as a "sensible fact," and even afterward, effort is required. In the beginning of *The Synthesis of Yoga*, Sri Aurobindo says: "The development of the experience in its rapidity, its amplitude, the intensity and power of its results, depends primarily, in the beginning of the path and long after, on the aspiration and personal effort of the sadhaka" (Aurobindo 1974, *Synthesis,* 10:51). The same question, and a similar answer, arises in relation to using one's individual will. The will is a power of consciousness and until we can surrender to a higher will, feel it working, we can and should use individual will toward spiritual goals.

Rejection is an active use of the will to deny entry to such things as anger, restlessness, egotism, depresssion, physical desire, sloth, impatience, mental falsehood, or to throw them out if they have taken root. These movements disturb the consciousness and prevent the higher or divine from coming in. Rejection is ongoing; simply saying "no" once to such movements rarely if ever vanquishes them. They are universal forces and will return at every opportunity, at every relaxation or slip in one's sadhana.

Lapses or oscillations, in which one falls from a previously attained state, are common in yoga. Sri Aurobindo and the Mother were quite familiar with the difficulties in yoga, and the necessity of facing them squarely, using whatever means appropriate to deal with them. In a famous essay, Sri Aurobindo gives a sobering statement about what we are attempting: "Imagine not the way is easy; the way is long, arduous, dangerous, difficult. At every step is an ambush, at every turn a pitfall. A thousand seen or unseen enemies will start up against thee." He says, "Is immortality a plaything to be given lightly to a child or the divine life a prize without effort or the crown for a weakling?" (Aurobindo circa 1927, 12:155-156). The Integral Yoga is not passive; you have to throw yourself on the side of the Divine, and keep on doing so.

You have to throw yourself on the side of the Divine, and keep on doing so.

In rejecting what we see as wrong, however, we should not become preoccupied with flaws, problems, or difficulties to the point of becoming ascetic. The turn towards asceticism is natural, and supported by centuries of spiritual teachings. Sri Aurobindo begins *The Life Divine* with a description of this error: "through many centuries a great army of shining witnesses, saints and teachers have swelled always the same lofty and distant appeal—renunciation—the sole path of knowledge, acceptance of physical life the act of the ignorant, cessation from birth the right use of human birth" (Aurobindo 1974, *Life Divine*, 18:23). The Mother calls this equating of spirituality with asceticism a universal superstition, saying, "If you describe someone as a spiritual man or a spiritual woman, people at once think of one who does not eat or sits all day without moving, one who lives in a hut in great poverty, one who has given away all he had and keeps nothing for himself. . . .This is a mental construction which must be thrown down if you are to be free to see and follow the spiritual truth" (The Mother 1929, 3:53-54). The end point of rejection should be equanimity, so that "If you are to get something," she says, "you accept it, and if you are to give up the very same thing, you with an equal willingness leave it. . . with the same smile of equanimity" (The Mother 1929, 3:54).

Sri Aurobindo and Mother often counseled balance and moderation in relation to activities such as meditation, prayer, mantra, study and reading. Disciples were not encouraged to spend all day in meditation or reading, nor to push specific practices intensely. Forced practice comes from a mental decision or belief, and is carried out through straining. Although it is appealing in its one-pointedness, such straining often unbalances the being in an unhealthy way. The true method of this yoga is to open up to a higher consciousness so that it will direct the sadhana. Sri Aurobindo writes, "The sadhaka must become conscious that a force other than his own, a force transcending his egoistic endeavor and capacity, is at work in him and to this Power he learns progressively to submit himself and delivers up to it the charge of his Yoga" (Aurobindo 1974, *Synthesis,* 20:52).

Meditation is useful in opening the inner being; it develops the inward movement. In advising about meditation, Sri Aurobindo and the Mother would often point to two general methods. Each has a specific purpose. The first is to go within, to the

106

heart; its purpose is to connect with the soul. The soul, the psychic, can then become a reliable guide for the rest of life and sadhana, steering one in the right direction in all things. When this connection has been established, the remainder of spiritual experience, though it will still be varied, need not be difficult or problematic. The second general method is to concentrate above the head, in order to bring down the higher, divine consciousness. This descent is characteristic of the Integral Yoga. In practice it can involve the descent of peace, light, force, bliss, knowledge.

This transformation does not come by contemplation alone; works are necessary, yoga in action is indispensable.

Meditation is important in that it develops the habit and power of going within and of being open to the higher consciousness, but it doesn't have the exclusive importance here which it is given in some other spiritual paths. Sri Aurobindo writes "The object of the sadhana is opening of the consciousness to the Divine and the change of the nature. Meditation or contemplation is one means to this but only one means; *bhakti* is another; work is another . . . this transformation does not come by contemplation alone; works are necessary, yoga in action is indispensable" (Aurobindo 1974, *Letters,* 22:526).

Yoga in particular, among spiritual paths, carries a connotation of intensity and extremism. Practices such as meditating all day, holding awkward postures for long periods of time, unusual purifications, chanting for hours, and forced breathing all contribute to this atmosphere. Sri Aurobindo and the Mother discovered, on the contrary, that the foundation for yoga is found in basic healthy qualities. Face every situation with cheerfulness, rather than allow a plodding gloominess. Keep on the path with a steady perseverance, instead of having excited enthusiasm followed by despair. Practice quietness of mind. Nurture a simple aspiration. Be patient when events don't turn out as planned. Keep a basic faith in the principles of yoga. Widen the mind to allow fresh ideas, and the emotions to include more and more of humanity.

Healthy qualities will often carry us through difficult situations, and keep us steady until a more complete mastery or integration is achieved. One difficulty with yoga is that it has unexpected results or experiences, often as a result of the very practice of yoga itself. We become obsessed with our limitations, sins, or flaws; we mishandle the higher consciousness, as the Mother noted, and become unbalanced; we oscillate between intense practice and blank, flat states where there is no light, no understanding, no energy for yoga at all. In an Integral Yoga, a quiet, steady, cheerful perseverance is immensely valuable.

One aspect of yoga is to develop the true qualities of each part of ourselves; each has qualities that can be strengthened, as a help toward success in the yoga

(l-r) Dr. Haridas Chaudhuri, Bina Chaudhuri,
& Rudolph Schaffer in Chinatown, San Francisco, 1952

*2650 Fulton Street, San Francisco,
which CIF occupied beginning 1955*

*Dr. Haridas Chaudhuri
teaching a class at CIF, late 1950s*

Bina Chaudhuri

Dr. Haridas Chaudhuri and Lama Govinda Anagarika

Images
from
the Ashram

Dr. Amit Goswami

Justine and Michael Tomms

111

Dr. Haridas Chaudhuri, meditating, 1958

Dr. Rudolph Schaffer, 1958

(l-r) Consul General Mr. & Mrs. Bajpai, CIF
Mahatma Gandhi birthday celebration, 1968; Dr. Haridas
& Bina Chaudhuri; Sant Keshavadas; Marjorie Watson
(seated far right); Ramamata Keshavadas

(l-r) Dr. Rina Sircar, Dr. Anne Teich, & Bina Chaudhuri at CIIS presentation of honorary doctorate to Vern Haddick, 1988

(l-r) Unknown, Ravi Shankar, Ketaki Kusari (sister of Karabi Sen), Bina Chaudhuri

The late Lillian Foote (top right) leading
carols at CIF Christmas party, early 1990s

(l-r) The late Lillian Foote, Vern haddick,
Bina Chaudhuri, & Paul Herman
at memorial for Dionne Marx, 1996

*Ramen Chakrabarti officiating at
annual CIF Durga Puja, late 1990s*

*Dr. Vishwanath Naravane, annual
Mahatma Gandhi birthday celebration, 2000*

Proclamation

City and County of San Francisco

WHEREAS, on behalf of the City and County of San Francisco, and in celebration of the Cultural Integration Fellowship's 50th anniversary this year, I commend their accomplishments and service; and

WHEREAS, San Francisco is comprised of people from many different cultures and ethnicities, and the Cultural Integration Fellowship has been a pioneer in sponsoring multi-cultural awareness with an appreciation for all religions; and

WHEREAS, the Cultural Integration Fellowship has provided one of the earliest pulpits for some of the first Indian and other Asian scholars and philosophers to speak the truths of their cultures and begin dialog that fosters mutual trust and appreciation; and

WHEREAS, they are a "parent" organization of the California Institute of Asian Studies; and

WHEREAS, through the work of the Cultural Integration Fellowship the children of San Francisco will grow up with an understanding of the value of diversity as our communities continue to become more diverse; now

THEREFORE BE IT RESOLVED, that I, Willie L. Brown, Jr., Mayor of the City and County of San Francisco, commend the Cultural Integration Fellowship for outstanding service, and do hereby proclaim April 15, 2001 as...

CULTURAL INTEGRATION DAY IN SAN FRANCISCO!

IN WITNESS WHEREOF, I have hereunto set my hand and caused the Seal of the City and County of San Francisco to be affixed.

Willie Lewis Brown, Jr.
Mayor

Proclamation (2001)

Dr. Rina Sircar & World Peace Musical Troupe,
CIF celebration of Buddha's birthday, 2001

Ling Wu (daughter of CIIS faculty member
Dr. Yi Wu) playing Gu zheng (Chinese harp) at
memorial for Dr. Haridas Chaudhuri, 1996

*(l-r) Aushim Chaudhuri, Alla Rakkha
and students, 1970*

Swara Samrat Dr. Ali Akbar Khan
Padma Vibhushan

28 February 2001

TO: Dilip Basu - 831-429-6671

FROM: Ali Akbar Khan - 415-456-5963

(To be read at the 50th Anniversary Inaugural Banquet on 3rd March)

Dear friends and members of the Cultural Integration Fellowship,

I am sorry that I am unable to be here with you today, but I am sending my heartfelt congratulations on the occasion of the 50th anniversary of the founding of your great organization. I knew your founder, Sri Haridas Chaudhuri, very well, and his wife, Shrimati Bina Chaudhuri, is a dear friend. Together, over the years, they worked hard to create an organization that continues to play a very important part as a major center of East-West relationships. Congratulations on a job well done!

With my best wishes for continued success,

Ali Akbar Khan

*Letter from Ali Akbar Kahn
on CIF's fiftieth anniversary*

121

Dr. Haridas Chaudhuri at home
(360 Cumberland Street, San Francisco), early 1970

of transformation. Since the goal of this yoga is to transform, the details of the process become important in the working out of that goal.

We are talking about pragmatic strengths and qualities, not moral virtues; the mind can become clear, the emotions deep and strong, the body fit to receive higher force. Sri Aurobindo describes these qualities in the chapter of *The Synthesis of Yoga* titled "The Power of the Instruments." These were delineated by Sri Aurobindo as part of the overall step of extending and raising the capacity of one's powers. For the body, it should accustom itself to respond to the mind and will, and then to the consciousness beyond the mind. It should also develop its capacity, *dharana*, for holding these higher energies. For our vital energy, the ability to sustain activity and work should be strong, not easily fatigued. It should acquire a four-fold quality of "Fullness, clear purity and gladness, equality, capacity for possession and enjoyment" (Aurobindo 1974, *Synthesis,* 21:707). The emotional part of us should have strength as well as sweetness, a will to universal good, and the power for universal love. For the thinking mind, it should develop "Purity, clear radiance, rich and flexible variety, integral capacity" (Aurobindo 1974, *Synthesis,* 21:710).

The endpoint of this development leads into the universality of the spirit. "These things are the ordinary aspects of the soul while it is working out its force in nature, but when we get nearer to our inner selves, then we get too a glimpse and experience of something which was involved in these forms and can disengage itself and stand behind and drive them, as if a general Presence or Power brought to bear on the particular working of this living and thinking machine. This is the force of the soul itself presiding over and filling the powers of its nature" (Aurobindo 1974, *Synthesis,* 21:721).

Every spiritual effort has an implicit understanding of the world and humanity. If this yoga sees positive value in certain movements of consciousness, and envisions some kind of transformation of these movements into higher forms, then what is the overall structure, the psychology of the whole being that the yoga uses? Sri Aurobindo devotes a chapter to this towards the end of *The Synthesis of Yoga*. He writes that we are "a spirit using the mind, life and body for an individual and communal experience" (Aurobindo 1974, 21:598). Not only that, but there is a further "instrument," called the Supermind, which is "in its very grain a consciousness and power of the Infinite" (Aurobindo 1974, 19:965).

Supermind, mind, life and body are the four instruments the spirit uses for its manifestation in the workings of Nature.

"Supermind, mind, life and body are the four instruments the spirit uses for its manifestation in the workings of Nature. Supermind is spiritual consciousness acting as a self-luminous knowledge, will, sense, aesthesis, energy, self-creative and unveiling power of its own delight and being. Mind is the action of the same powers, but limited and only very indirectly and partially illumined." (Aurobindo 1974, 21:599)

Even though the spirit is infinite, it identifies itself "in the frontal active part of its consciousness"

(Aurobindo 1974, 21:602). with a limited form that arises in the space of a single lifetime. The power of consciousness to transform one, mentioned at the beginning of this talk, enables us to move beyond our particular form; consciousness can break through and beyond it, break it up or develop it, select, reject, new-create, reveal out of itself a greater self-formulation. What it believes itself to be by the whole active will of its consciousness in its instruments, that it is or tends to become, *yo yacchraddhah sa eva sah:* what it believes it can be and has full faith in becoming, that it changes to in nature, evolves or discovers. (Aurobindo 1974, 21:602)

Our thoughts, emotions, even our body, are only frontal pieces, while behind this front, there lies an inner mind and consciousness. This inner being is much wider, and has direct contact with other persons, other forces, other worlds. When we awaken to the inner being, we become conscious here, which is why Sri Aurobindo calls it the "subliminal" rather than the subconscious: it is behind a veil, not below consciousness. Sadhana done on the surface is limited, a matter of guesswork, hopes, tentative aspiration, whereas once the inner being opens sadhana becomes exact, direct, effective.

In their explorations, Sri Aurobindo and the Mother discovered that the complete evolution of the individual involves three broad transformations. These are different from realizations of the Divine.

The first is the psychic transformation, finding the soul, opening up one's life to it more and more, allowing it to guide every aspect of life and *sadhana.* The second is the spiritual transformation, opening the consciousness to the higher and Divine, breaking the bounds of the ego and entering into the transcendence of the self, broadening out into the cosmic awareness. The psychic and the spiritual transformations have been known through history, though under other names.

The third is the supramental transformation. The founders of this path achieved what could be called an avataric feat, in finding and bringing down this hitherto unknown element into the life and evolution of the world. Speaking about this final transformation is problematic, simply because it presupposes so much else before it. Even reading about it is often akin to listening to Morse code: fascinating, but unintelligible.

Sri Aurobindo and Mother saw that there was something more than the inner being, more than the higher awareness, more than the essential Divine consciousness; they saw a level of divine consciousness that has not been previously accessible to humanity. This Supermind or gnostic consciousness is practically indescribable; it proceeds from and is always in complete harmony with Divine reality. "Light is [there] one with Force, the vibrations of knowledge with the rhythm of the will and both are one, perfectly and without seeking, groping or effort, with the assured result." Aurobindo, as quoted in Van Vrekhem (1997, p. 61).

A common idea about spirituality is that the inner life has always been the same, that the realizations of the spiritual teachers of the past are eternally valid and binding. And there is a truth to this. But the founders of this yoga saw that there is a spiritual evolution to the world as a whole, and they found that a crucial link needed to be built between this Supermind and the physical world. That work took place over decades, and has many dramatic stages and unexpected aspects. But the upshot is that the thing was done: according to them, this element, this golden "X," is now here, active, available to us all.

Herein lies the crux of the work that they did over the last century, and it is easy to see how, as Georges Van Vrekhem writes, "This subject may appear fantastic and unbelievable to the unprepared" (Van Vrekhem 1997, 111). We are talking about what is known in India as an avatar, a person who does something universal for the advancement of all of humanity.

> *They also saw that there could evolve an entirely new species beyond humanity. . . [a] vision of the emergence of new species, based on a truly divine consciousness.*

They also saw that there could evolve an entirely new species beyond humanity. Think of a perfect technological utopia, where all problems of disease, of pollution, of society are solved; imagine that unthinkably powerful computers work hand in hand with humanity to advance our knowledge and wisdom; visualize a world where progress is on-going, where the best is continually getting better. But now base that vision on the emergence of new species, based on a truly divine consciousness, and you have some idea of what this yoga looks forward to.

Sri Aurobindo described this "new creation" briefly in the middle of his epic poem, *Savitri.*

There was no sob of suffering anywhere
Experience ran from point to point of joy:
Bliss was the pure undying truth of things.

127

All Nature was a conscious front of God:
A wisdom worked in all, self-moved, self-sure,
A plenitude of illimitable Light,
An authenticity of intuitive Truth,
A glory and passion of creative Force.
Infallible, leaping from eternity,
The moment's thought inspired the passing act.
A word, a laughter, sprang from Silence' breast,
A rhythm of Beauty in the calm of Space,
A knowledge in the fathomless heart of Time.

The senses there were outlets of the soul;
Even the youngest child-thought of the mind
Incarnated some touch of highest things.
There substance was a resonant harp of self,
A net for the constant lightnings of the spirit,
A magnet power of love's intensity
Whose yearning throb and adoration's cry
Drew God's approaches close, sweet, wonderful.
Its solidity was a mass of heavenly make;
Its fixity and sweet permanence of charm
Made a bright pedestal for felicity.
Its bodies woven by a divine sense
Prolonged the nearness of soul's clasp with soul;
Its warm play of external sight and touch
Reflected the glow and thrill of the heart's joy,
Mind's climbing brilliant thoughts, the spirit's
     bliss;
Life's rapture kept for ever its flame and cry.
All that now passes lived immortal there
In the proud beauty and fine harmony
Of Matter plastic to spiritual light.
Its ordered hours proclaimed the eternal Law;
Vision reposed on a safety of deathless forms;
Time was Eternity's transparent robe.
An architect hewing out self's living rock,

Phenomenon built Reality's summer-house
On the beaches of the sea of Infinity.
(Aurobindo 1974, *Savitri,* 28:324-325, 328-329)

REFERENCES

Chaudhuri, Haridas. 1968. *Mastering the Problems of Living.* Secaucus, NJ: Citadel Press.
Aurobindo. 1974. Letters on Yoga, Aurobindo Birth Centenary Library (SABCL), vols. 22, 23. Pondicherry, India: Sri Aurobindo Ashram.
_____ 1974. *On Himself.* SABCL, vol. 26.
_____ 1974. *The Life Divine,* SABCL, vols. 18, 19.
_____ 1974. *The Synthesis of Yoga,* SABCL, vols. 20, 21.
_____ 1974. *Savitri,* SABCL, vol. 28.
_____ circa 1927. *Essays Divine and Human,* The Complete Works of Aurobindo, vol. 12. Pondicherry, India: Sri Aurobindo Ashram.
The Mother. 1929. *Questions and Answers,* Complete Works of the Mother (CWM), vols. 3, 5, 6, 7. Pondicherry, India: Sri Aurobindo Ashram.
Van Vrekhem, Georges. 1997. *Beyond Man, The Life and Work of Aurobindo and the Mother.* New Delhi: HarperCollins India.

David Hutchinson is President of the Aurobindo Association, and associate editor of *Collaboration,* a journal of Integral Yoga in America.

PART II

TRIBUTES

Dr. Chaudhuri

by Lillian Foote

An advertisement in the Church Services section of the newspaper that said "Universal Religion" attracted me to the Cultural Integration Fellowship on Easter Sunday morning in 1968 where I listened to what I thought was the most moving Easter talk that I had ever heard. The speaker was Dr. Haridas Chaudhuri and to my astonishment—an Indian. His talk seemed to open great vistas of insight and so much light that I sought out more and more of his discourses. At that time he was giving Tuesday night classes which were open to the public, and then through brochures I discovered the newly founded California Institute of Asian Studies (CIAS) and began to become involved there too. Once a month a meditation was held at the Fellowship which was followed by a question period. Those were great learning experiences, for no matter what the questions, Dr. Chaudhuri could develop an insight that expanded your consciousness and made you hungry for more.

He talked of the latent divinity in every human being, of the indwelling divine guru, and of the love that would transform one's life. "All men are essentially children of God—one supreme principle which is self-shining like the sun." "Love is the essence of one's being," he said, then illustrated with a story. He was a master storyteller, and laced his talks with poignant stories. Here is one example:

A young student went to his yogi to ask how to find Truth. "The Truth is that you are one with Brahman," advised the yogi. That gave him the feeling of great power. On his way down the path he saw an elephant coming. Now I shall use my power and command the elephant to stop, he thought, but the elephant kept on coming. "Stand aside," shouted the driver. The student did not move, whereupon the elephant lifted him from the path and set him aside. The student was humiliated and complained to his yogi. "But the elephant is also Brahman," said the yogi. "Why did you not stand aside?"

Dr. Chaudhuri warned of the danger of power and of lopsided spirituality. Wisdom and love are inseparable. If wisdom is divorced from love it degenerates into intellectualism. We need to protect the spirit of love in our hearts with the voice of thunder and there are occasions in life when one has to do this.

The subject of non-attachment sometimes came up. We become attached to money, food, position, desires, certain behaviors, etc. Dr. Chaudhuri's message was: to play your part to the best of your ability and leave all consequences in the hands of Providence. One has no control over consequences anyway. Whether you succeed or fail is not important so long as you have played your part according to your inner vision. How he demonstrated this truth is unforgettable. The permit for the school's occupation of the building at 21st and Dolores Streets was expiring and we wished to renew it. There was some opposition among a few persons in the community, but it was not considered serious. Nevertheless, we thought we were well prepared when we met before the commission. We lost! And filed out with heavy hearts and hangdog expressions. But not Dr. Chaudhuri. He was already looking for an official who could support the next step to be taken. It was one of the big lessons of my life. No energy there for blame or excuse, commiseration or despair. As you know, we continued to occupy the building.

Love is the essence of one's being.

Dr. Chaudhuri was a great pragmatist: "The kind of experiences you have depend on your liver and your bank account." He was also a reconciler and a harmonizer. There were always the good guys and the bad guys—the gods and the demons. In international relations we think of the other side as the bad guys. But no group is all good or all bad. Every group has both. We may have our own group which is good for our growth, but, he warned, remember that your own group is not the only "court appointed" group in all the world.

We talked of the crisis of identity and likened it to a boy in an orphanage who felt rejected and lonely and suffered in isolation. When he discovered that his uncle in another country had bequeathed him a legacy, he was "a somebody" and his own life

132

changed. In our ordinary life we live and move in a false identity and suffer fears and anxieties. That is living in an orphanage. You have forgotten that your true father is Emperor of the Universe. But it doesn't end there: a lot of doing is necessary. If a boy abuses his inheritance, he may lose it all. He needs to bring all his resources—body, life, and mind—to bear on making his inheritance productive.

When life is filled with joy
it is full of creative action.

Nonduality was another important subject. In the West we have been in the habit of separating the body from the spirit, the sacred from the profane. Dr. Chaudhuri taught that the entire universe is a manifestation of God, that nothing can be excluded, that while man is essentially a spark of the divine, he must have a passport from nature to enter the kingdom of the spirit.

Dr. Chaudhuri's discourses on Creative Action were absolutely brilliant. It was the sum and substance of his life. "When life is filled with joy, it is full of creative action." Life is a process of change; we must not remain in fixation, but break through the barriers. Great wisdom is required because change can go forward or backward. The secret of going forward is in unconditional self surrender. "Let Thy will, not mine be done." Irrational forces are at work, but in the heart of man lies a great creative impulse, a creative freedom which is the essence of the human soul. Life is like a blank canvas or a huge block of marble that you can take into your own hands and fashion by the spirit within you, and something meaningful can emerge. The great mission of man is to fashion the raw material of the soul and transform it into a thing of beauty.

Dr. Chaudhuri was a gentle and loving human being, a brilliant scholar, a humble person, and extremely self-disciplined. He believed in balance and moderation. While outwardly soft, inside there was a power-house. The light that was within shed its radiance on all.

The late *Lillian Foote* was for thirty years an enthusiastic supporter of both the Cultural Integration Fellowship and California Institute of Asian (Integral) Studies. She served on the boards of trustees of both organizations through many terms.

A Rare Person

by Lyne Duchamp

As a student and a disciple of Dr. Haridas Chaudhuri, I find it very difficult to put down in words a realistic and worthy expression of a man of that caliber. A brilliant scholar, an eloquent and magnetic orator, an outstanding philosopher—all the above assets and many more are already well known through his work and reputation.

My first contact with Dr. Chaudhuri took place at the CIF in 1965 where I went on a Sunday morning attracted by the subject "Cosmic Consciousness" to be presented at the Sunday Service. As I was there early, I could see the room gradually filling up to capacity. Unable to find room inside, some people sat on the floors outside the conference room. The atmosphere was one of great expectation.

Then as the speaker proceeded unfolding his subject, I was impressed by his magnetic personality as well as the content of his speech, presented in a crystal clear fashion, tempered with a sense of humor which put everyone at ease.

This master of the podium was stirring out of my inner self values and concepts with which I had not been in touch before. From then on I looked forward to his next lecture. Later on I became one of his students at the California Institute of Asian Studies.

Dr. Haridas Chadhuri had the great gift to reach everyone in his audience. His subjects disclosing profound truths and concepts, illustrated and reinforced with relevant allegories, appealed and touched every phase of one's inner being. Dr. Chaudhuri was one of those rare persons one is fortunate to meet in the course of a lifetime.

The date when he suddenly left us the world grew darker. A bright light had gone out of our horizon. However, his spirit was, and is, still with us, will continue to live in us, and among us, and will never be extinguished.

Lyne Duchamp was by profession a nurse in the intensive care unit of San Francisco's French Hospital. By vocation she was a singer, committed student on the path of spiritual development, and author of an insightful volume on psychosomatic medicine.

Memories of Dr. Chaudhuri

by Theodosia T. Greene

I think it was the 1963 article in the *San Francisco Chronicle* that first caught my eye. A birthday celebration for Sri Aurobindo—complete with Indian gourmet refreshments—was to be held on my very own August birthday! Since nobody was baking me a cake, this was surely an editorial Finger of Fate. The gods came in delicious disguises of *pakoras*, *puris*, and *papadams*. Little did I suspect that this first meeting with Dr. Chaudhuri would provide a lifetime of spiritual nourishment.

I sat in the front row for his Sunday lecture. It seemed as if I had known him forever. It seemed as if he was speaking words which filled inner spaces left gnawingly empty by my Southern Baptist upbringing. Instead of their plea to join the Christian women's bake-off, he urged, "Inner illumination without active dedication to the good of humanity is unfinished business." And "The integral poise of consciousness enables man to grasp the timeless mystery of Being, as well as the meaning of Time." I was consumed with burning curiosity to learn about "the authentic Self," "transcendental consciousness," "the undifferentiated and unpolarized presentation continuum of a baby," "sunyata," and I was particularly attracted to "the effortless growth from within."

After ten years of Dr. Chaudhuri's gentle and inspiring instruction, I moved to Southern California for business reasons but would visit him in his office whenever I returned to the Bay Area. One such occasion made an unforgettable impact. Without words, he illustrated our potential for direct contact with luminous, nontemporal Being.

It was one of those shining-blue days for which San Francisco is famous. Flags fluttering in the brisk breeze, salt crystal air, and green foliage in full leaf. I knocked on his door and entered. His desk was piled high with papers. After we exchanged friendly greetings and information, he unburdened to me all the problems facing the Institute: accreditation difficulties, financial worries, the city's mistakenly identifying them with a flaky religious cult, an irksome investigation from the fire department, etc. His brows knit and his visage darkened as he recounted all the numerous troubles. Concerned and disheartened, I sighed and shook my head sympathetically. Suddenly, he brightened and burst into laughter. He swung back in his chair and roared, tears of hilarity rolling down his cheeks.

I stared at him. What was this? Had he flipped?

Then I understood. Inside that office, the air had become thick with material problems; gloom and doom had descended. Yet, in the higher form of the sage's viewpoint to know things as they ARE, the sun was shining, peace and prosperity pervaded our land, Sri Hari and his family were healthy, and I was happy to be with my old friend and beloved teacher again. Ananda.

Theodosia T. Greene, from her home in Sedona, Arizona, has been a long-time and generous supporter of CIF.

138

Our Neighborhood Ashram

by Helen Desai

Over forty years ago my husband Raj and I discovered the San Francisco ashram, the Cultural Integration Fellowship. "Perfect! It's right in our neighborhood," we agreed. We had moved from Jamshedpur, India, with our baby daughter Monica to San Francisco in 1958. Raj had found an engineering job in San Francisco and we were exploring the Richmond District, our new neighborhood.

Cultural Integration was already important to Raj and me. Raj and I were married in 1954; he was "East" (from Mumbai, India) and I was "West" (from Santa Ana, California). Since we both came from liberal and loving families, we were both open to experiencing and learning from the world, within our traditions and without. We wanted to sip the nectar of spiritual wisdom of all great teachers, past and present. How fortuitous that the CIF was within walking distance!

Early on we became friends of the Chaudhuri family. We remember Dr. Haridas Chaudhuri as a warm-hearted, gentle, smiling, and kind philosopher whose insightful lectures illuminated our hearts and minds. Over the decades we met together, not only at the Ashram, but also at other cultural, social and educational venues. Some of our dear teachers and gurus we first met at the Ashram. Shivaram, one of Kerala's greatest classical dancers was a teacher at the Ashram. I and other members of our family benefited from his dance and yoga classes. Sant Keshavadas was another great teacher whom we first met at the Ashram. His storytelling and musical genius and his deep bhakti yoga were irresistible. My first Sanskrit teacher was Dr. Saraswati Mishra, who got his start at CIF. In recent years, Bina, Raj and I have studied Sanskrit with one of Dr. Mishra's disciples, Ma Bhaskarananda, and Bharati Ma. During the 40-plus years many exceptional personalities have come through the open doors of CIF and into our hearts: Haridas and Bina and their children; Shivaram, Sant Keshavadas, Dr. Mishra, Uday Sengupta, Rudolph Schaffer, Dr. Vishwanath Naravane, and many, many other good friends.

From its beginning the CIF has promoted the integration of the cultural and spiritual values of all peoples to achieve world harmony. There is a story to illustrate this multiplicity in unity. It is said that a Chinese sage known as "the noble-minded Fu," when asked whether he was a Buddhist priest, pointed to his Taoist cap; when asked whether he was a Taoist, pointed to his Confucian shoes: and finally, being asked whether he was a Confucian, pointed to his Buddhist scarf. In a similar way the Ashram has provided the freedom for me to weave the various-colored threads of Vedanta, Unitarian, Brahma Kumaris' raja yoga, Gurumayi siddha yoga, and Gaia-Ecology in my life's journey.

The Ashram celebrated its fiftieth anniversary in 2001. With such a vision for world harmony, with such a wonderful group of people, with Bina's leadership, the Ashram will flourish. May it flourish for the next hundred years! May its philosophy of the brotherhood/sisterhood of all beings of this earth light our paths in ever widening rays!

Helen Desai and her husband Raj have served many terms on the boards of trustees of both the Cultural Integration Fellowship and the California Institute of Integral Studies. Helen has had a lifelong experience of both Indian and American cultures, which she has shared in San Francisco as an instructor of art history, docent of museum collections, and founder of the Society for Art and Cultural History of India.

Haridas Chaudhuri—Teacher For a New Age

by Robert Bainbridge

Sri Haridas Chaudhuri is alive and well and living in the hearts and minds of all who came within his ever-widening sphere of influence as a great-souled teacher.

A teacher of Dr. Chaudhuri's stature affects eternity. What finer expression of this ongoing participation in the spirit of this world than his observation that:

> every human being is essentially a child of immortality, a focalized expression of the vital urge. His purpose in life is to realize his authentic self as a unique center of creative freedom, as an active source of new values, as a channel of expression of the hidden possibilities of Being.

Dr. Chaudhuri was richly endowed with a transcendent vision of human destiny and a commitment to serve in the fields of human aspiration. He reached out to a hopeful world with transformative power to affect the quality of life and civilization. In his untiring adventure toward the fulfillment of the Eternal in time, he was an agent of evolution, an inspired pioneer in the inviting terrain of tomorrow's wide-open spaces.

Blessed indeed is that man who has found a life work to which he can devote his finer energies with satisfaction and joy. Twice blessed are those who have recognized their calling and capacity as teacher to the world, for in its noblest dimensions the creative act of teaching spreads the seeds of an inexorable harvest in worlds yet unborn.

As teacher, Haridas Chaudhuri held out to seekers everywhere the noble promise of a transformation within humankind toward supraconscious selfhood and a unitary life of love and spiritual fellowship beyond the bonds of suffering, ignorance and separative striving. As teacher of an improved order of human life on earth, he worked toward liberation of the learner's capacities and powers in natural and spontaneous ways.

In examining the patterns of life which hold the individual in the bondage of familiarity and security, he contributed to an environment which encouraged his students to be self-aware and to understand the promptings and aspirations of their own unfolding Divinity. Together with his students and disciples he explored the uncharted domain of Ultra-Man, as universal adventurers of inner space seeking to open up untapped frontiers of the human intellect and spirit. In the words of Lucretius:

> Him noise of Gods, nor lightnings, nor the roar
> Of raging heavens subdued, but pricked the
>   more
> His spirit's valiance, till he longed the Gate
> To burst of this low prison of man's fate.
> And thus the living ardor of his mind
> Conquered and clove its way, he passed behind
> The world's last flaming well, and through the
>   whole
> Of space uncharted ranged his mind and soul.

Dr. Chaudhuri's aspirations, unfolding through his powerful words and pen, invested his teaching with an animating life and spirit that elicited a student's higher nature and helped to transmute mundane affairs into experiences of meaning and self-discovery. He provided quiet invitation to live each moment consistent with one's finest vision and highest ideals.

Haridas Chadhuri shared abundantly the elixir of a creative energy and quality of self that endures as a vibrant teaching force beyond the reaches of time and place, mind and emotion, and the restricted power of words alone. Indeed, he created around himself an ecology that made possible a life of becoming and self-giving. Because he lived, daily extending the horizons of his own spirit as a seedman of unbounded tomorrows, other human beings have moved more surely toward fuller self-realization too.

But even a great teacher's ideals and teachings can quicken the pulse of humanity in enduring fashion only in relation to the quality of response evidenced in the lives of those who come to learn. Sri Haridas taught by example that knowledge without action is empty, and he stressed that the best education teaches that the end of knowledge is service. Surely those of us who walk in his wake can offer no greater tribute than to take up the torch where he has passed it on and to enter more surely the arena of cosmic mystery and wonder that so inspired his genius.

Great teachers have appeared in every era to light the way for those capable of responding to their example and teachings. Haridas Chaudhuri was one of them, a living synthesis of life and spirit, knowledge and action, wisdom and compassion. By participating fully in the challenges and opportunities of everyday life, he became an agent of conscious evolution in the rhythm of universal existence. Like all great teachers, he will live on long after the physical form is gone, "woven into the stuff of other men's lives."

After he came to San Francisco, the late *Professor Bainbridge* was one of the earliest graduates from CIAS with a doctoral degree supervised by Dr. Chaudhuri.

Rudolph Schaffer
Benefactor to the Chaudhuri Family
and East-West Studies

by Bina Chaudhuri

Note: Mrs. Bina Chaudhuri delivered this tribute at the celebration of Rudolph Schaffer's hundredth birthday.

All the elements have to be in rhythm." These words, which belong to my dear friend, Dr. Rudolph Schaffer, express a fundamental truth. Their concept is as simple as the single seed which grows into a tree and whose fruit, in turn, produces an entire glade. In the roots and branches of such a glade, a whole population of animals, birds, insects and smaller plants finds the nourishment of home. And through migration and pollination the fruits of this community spread outward, and so connect with that far greater network which is the planet.

"All the elements have to be in rhythm." What a wonderful recognition! If I have been using a flowery metaphor, it is because Rudolph Schaffer's vision has been just such a seed. It has flowered and prospered and spread. And it has provided—and continues to provide—much nourishment for all of us.

I first met Rudolph when I came to San Francisco in 1952 to join my husband, who had come to the United States from India to teach at the American Academy of Asian Studies. At Rudolph's invitation, we lived in his home. My husband, Haridas, lectured at his School of Design, along with many other pioneers of what we now call East-West studies, such as Chingwah Lee, Chiang Yee and Lewis McRitchie. It was at Rudolph's school at 350 Union St., that Haridas founded the Cultural Integration Fellowship.

This involvement, and Rudolph's deep friendship and wisdom, proved vital throughout my husband's work here, with the Fellowship, and in founding the California Institute of Asian Studies, which has evolved into the California Institute of Integral Studies.

In 1951 Rudolph's school was already twenty-five years old. His work as an artist, as a teacher, and as a philosopher of life and aesthetics, was already internationally known. His reputation as one of the truly transformative figures in the twentieth century was already secure, but as we can all see now, he was really just getting started. So I want to celebrate today not simply the wonders of the first century of Rudolph Schaffer, and to wish him the happiest of birthdays, but to celebrate also the fruits we have to look forward to in the future. For the seed of his great vision continues to grow.

Dr. Rudolph Frederick Schaffer has given us color. I mean that literally. He has changed the way in which we both live in and see the world. In introducing aniline dyes to building materials, such as wood, plaster and sheet rock, to candle wax, and to textiles, Rudolph opened up the palette of everyday life. He also introduced the color warp into weaving. In part, these accomplishments combined

147

the wisdom of the artist with the knowledge of a scientist, a theory of color combined with the practical application of chemistry. Much more importantly, it proved to be an integration of the mind and the heart with the eye.

It is this integration, which is also a union of East and West, and of spirituality with daily life, which is Rudolph's greatest lesson: all of the elements have to be in rhythm.

Rudolph Schaffer was born on June 26, 1886, and raised on a farm in Clare, Michigan. His family home there is now recognized as an historic monument, and he has remained an active force in that community. Not long ago, he established a children's library there.

As a child, he studied music avidly, learned to model clay from a neighbor, and gathered wildflowers with his friends. Such early activities have remained central to this day. Indeed, even before he began college at the Detroit Normal Training School in 1907, where he formally studied to teach arts and crafts, Rudolph had worked for two years as a teacher in a rural Michigan country school.

In 1908, on a summer vacation, Rudolph took his first trip to Europe, where he saw first-hand the great monuments and craft-works of the Western tradition: By 1910, he had begun teaching in a very different form of the West—in Pasadena. Already, the crafts movement had sprung up in California as an alternative to the colorless products then being endlessly manufactured in the industrial centers of the Eastern United States.

Rudolph was immediately recognized as a master in his field. He was selected by the U.S. Commissioner of Education in 1914 as one of 125 manual arts teachers to visit Germany, to inspect the state of European industrial design education. On this trip, while in Vienna, Rudolph met the architect Josef Hoffmann. Hoffmann was then involved with a school called the Wiener Werkstatte, through which he created not only his designs for buildings, but all of the elements which went into them, right down to the dishes and formal wear for the occupants. This concept of a visually integrated life made great sense to Rudolph, and its manifestation through the form of a school inspired him. Teaching might not only be a natural inclination and talent, as well as a means of making a living, it might prove also to be the most effective means available to bring all the elements of life into rhythm.

The first result of Rudolph's new revelation was that he lost his job as a teacher in Pasadena, by overstaying his time in Vienna beyond the start of the academic year. Although he might not have realized it at that time, this was an extraordinarily happy accident, for it provided him with both the opportunity and impetus to move north to the Bay Area, which was to become the site of his greatest work. At first he lived in Piedmont and taught in the Oakland and Hayward public schools. Later he taught at the University of California, Berkeley, and at the school which is now the California College of Arts and Crafts. Then, in 1917, he began teaching at the forerunner of the San Francisco Art Institute. Finally, after another tour of Europe with two friends, Raymond Duncan and Mark Tobey, who both went on to become artists of world renown (it was also during this trip that Rudolph discovered the Indian dancer Uday Shanker), he opened the Rudolph Schaffer School of Rhythmo-Chromatic Design in San Francisco, in 1926.

During this same period, Rudolph was extraordinarily active in many art forms: flower arranging, interior design and display, and creating sets and costumes for theaters throughout the Bay Area, including the Greek Theater and Wheeler Auditorium in Berkeley, and the new Civic Auditorium in San Francisco. His collaborations for the theater with Norman Edwards were exhibited internationally. In 1935, Rudolph published the first folio in America on flower arranging. He was by now one of the defining figures in the rapidly evolving culture of the San Francisco region. The original seed of his vision had grown as tall as a redwood.

One aspect of this influence which I naturally find to be of the greatest importance, has been his impact on interest in Asian art, and on the useful integration of Eastern perspectives into Western culture. While Rudolph began studying and collecting Asian art well before he started his school, it was at the school's second location, on St. Anne's Street on Nob Hill, that he opened the East-West Gallery and began alternating shows of Oriental art with shows of art from the West. Actually, I don't know of an earlier use of the phrase "East-West" in this sense, and it has occurred to me that Rudolph may have invented that also. It wouldn't surprise me one bit.

The integration of Asian art, culture, and philosophy were central to the mission of Rudolph's school from the very beginning. Here was a tradition in which the spiritual dimension was recognized as an aspect of all things, and in which art was fully incorporated into daily life. At the heart of all the great Asian religions, we find the idea that all the elements must be in rhythm. As the Balinese say, "We have no art. We do everything as best we can."

Not surprisingly, Rudolph's school was his home even then. Its curriculum extended beyond pure rhythmo-chromatic color theory, textiles, interiors, architecture, and flower arranging. There was room for performance that could include avant-garde music and dance. And the school itself was an example, not only of Rudolph's great talent as a designer, but of the greater concept of art-in-life itself.

Out of Rudolph's school his students and those of Chingwah Lee (who taught at the school for two decades) formed the Asian Art Society, the group that established the Asian Art Museum in Golden Gate Park and brought the Avery Brundage Collection to San Francisco. Ten years ago, when Rudolph was still a young man of 90, the Asian Art Museum mounted a major exhibition of his extraordinary collection of Oriental art. He has served on their Acquisition and Exhibition committee and has donated important works to their permanent collection.

Decade after decade, from Pasadena in 1910, from the Bay Area since 1915, and from his own school from 1926 until it closed in 1984, Rudolph Schaffer trained the major designers of our region. Textile artist Dorothy Wright Liebes, Peter Roccia, president of the Wicker Works furniture company, architect John Garden Campbell, the late Don Smith and Paul Faria, who were responsible for design at Gump's for decades, and John Calori at I. Magnin's, are just some of those who have spread the seed of his thought, bringing rhythmo-chromatics and Rudolph's integral vision to millions of persons who may never have heard his name.

Two years ago, in an article on Rudolph in *California Living,* John Calori described the impact the Schaffer school had for him:

> Rudolph created a whole world at the school. I remember walking up the stairs that first day and through a gate to a totally

151

transformed world. When I decided that my talent was geared more to the immediate solutions in display design rather than the longer-range process of interior design, Rudolph and the faculty tailored my assignments to that goal. I was given the freedom to develop my own direction and I learned to merchandise display by applying the yin-yang positive-negative principles that governed Rudolph's whole existence.

Just as all these talented people, and the wonderful work of the Asian Art Museum itself, can be seen as seeds from Rudolph's tree, so can the California Institute of Integral Studies. In addition to the enormous help which Rudolph gave to my husband and myself when we first came to America, many of the Institute's original board members, its earliest close friends, were students of Rudolph Schaffer. In 1984, the Institute awarded him a doctoral degree in Philosophy and President John Broomfield subsequently appointed him Distinguished Professor of Art and Creativity Studies. Rudolph himself donated a Tang dynasty horse to the Institute and proceeds from its sale were used to establish the Rudolph Schaffer Chair in Art and Creativity Studies. Jack Weller, founding director of the Expressive Arts program at CIIS, was the first person to occupy the chair.

The idea that "all the elements have to be in rhythm" is a truth that does not age. It is a concept as old as spirituality, and as fresh in the modern world as its current expression in ecology.

So, Rudolph, I want to bless you and to thank you for your friendship, your leadership and for 100 years of extraordinary and wonderful work. Our present to you is to set for ourselves a goal—to accomplish over the next century what you have always done with such grace, charm and wisdom: "to teach the eyes, mind and heart to see."

PART III

A ROUND OF POETRY

Dr. Haridas Chaudhuri

by Joy Kapur

A manifestation of pure consciousness
Of divine origin and fame
Infinities of love, peace and culture
Abound his name.
Remembering him is soul's delight
And brings springs of ecstasy
Sent on this earth to fulfill some prophecy.

Around him we found heavenly aromas
And whispers of eternity.
He brought smile and sunshine
And healed the wounds of humanity.
Brilliance in his luminous eyes
Had starts of eternity.
The tenderness of his gaze
Mingled in Divine Grace
Had purity, serenity and ethereality.
Sent on a mission to enlighten the mind
Purify the heart, uplift the soul
And make us whole in a divine way.

You can see angels line up in heaven
To shower bounties on this day.

Mother India

by Helen Wallace

Note: Helen Wallace read and presented this poem at the Cultural Integration Fellowship on Dr. Chaudhuri's memorial concert day, June 2000.

Motherland of Europe's languages,
and in many ways, mother of us all:
You are the mother of our philosophy,
much of our mathematics,
and through Buddha and Krishna
the ideals embodied in Christianity.

You have some divine in you,
a touch that heals,
the OM-sound of God that penetrates
my whole being in a way sweet fragrance
is mingled in the rising smoke of sandalwood incense.

The purity of your mind is reflected
in the sacred white lotus; like the silvery moon
you radiate a cool light of peacefulness.

In my daily meditation, it is as though
I melt into the lotus of your heart,
to be filled with the joy of your love and peace.

155

Mother India, may the treasure of your divine wisdom bring service to the world and peace of mind to all lives.

Descent of the Mother Divine

by Durga Mukherjee

In this world of physical advent
Has anybody thought of life
Sprouting in the mystery of birth and death
To take the world out of strife?

Who thinks today of the Divine's secret game
As sages did in the past,
To know the cause of causes with His mind of frame?

Why this waste of time in such illusion,
By airing false pride of glory
Like a silk worm in a cocoon preparing for
    dissolution?

Being soaked in jealousy succulent
It enters the twigs of every branch
And spreads its wings all over to stop the light radiant
As if to fulfill devil's lusty crunch.

So many messiahs came to earth,
Ordained by the Divine Grace,
To provide humanity a suitable berth
For founding truth to win over the race;
Yet the earth has not moved an inch
From the grip of the sickening clinch.

Not even the advent of the Divine Mother on earth,
With pure soul and celestial sanctity,
Could deter the devil from its destructive path
What could be worse than this calamity?

With the passage of time
The new culture came to devour the earth
Thereby it fell from its own confidence
Taking the falsehood as berth.

The Divine Mother, not finding any place
to found the life of peace for humanity,
Left the earth with great reluctance,
To pity mankind from eternity.

Is there no salvation in this domain
From the clutch of satanic snake,
Full of greed and poison,
Polluting the globe in its wake?

Fear not, doubt not, forget not, the illusion
Created by the satanic force;
The Mother is again coming for salvation,
With the prayer of Aurobindo as a great source.

Slowly the effulgent cosmic flame
Has entered each skin-hole and atom of the planet
To reveal life's aim
And the Divine Soul in complete fulfillment.

With the vibration every where in the blue sky long,
And the revival of life in desert's tree
Comes the aroma of silent song
To tune human unity in that spree.

No more doubt, no more fear
With the hand of the Mother on the rudder
To protect Humankind with hallowed glow
After crossing an endless path
On the victory chariot with the radiant blow.

Oh humanity, awake and bow to the Mother,
Experience yearning fulfilled through her!

Durga Mukherjee was born into a spiritual family in
India, and his lifelong intellectual bent toward Indian
philosophy and spirit inspires him to try to understand divine omnipotence through the teachings of
Sri Aurobindo and the Mother.

Victory Day—The 24th November, 1926

by Durga Mukherjee

From the deep immeasurable space of Infinite
Comes the epiphany with vibrant Divine light,
Rushing from above with a pattern
Through strange symbols,
Full of expectation and aspiration.

Silence, absolute Silence everywhere
Outflowing with Divinity
To welcome the Great Mother with every benign
  dignity.

Mirra became the Mother on this auspicious day
With Auro's blessing, describing the event in a superb
  way:
It was Krishna's desire to bring Supramental force
Upon the earth concretely, actively, from all the
  available source.
Intensive work by both of them
Readied the ground to bring the Supramental frame.

Yet Aurobindo had to play his important role,
To achieve the Supramental, through his yoga, as a
  prime goal.
Krishna, as Avatar of overmind,
Had sent Aurobindo many times on earth

As Avatar and Supermind
To bring evolution with revolution at every stage of
  birth.

Buddha's love for humanity knew no bound,
As told by the Mother about his presence
Everywhere in the earth's atmosphere, in essence,
To keep his promise of liberation to humanity in
  credence
Even though it meant Sacrifice to "Nirvana" on this
  very ground.

To hasten the process of Supramental consciousness
Mother worked through the Master for everyone's
  steadfastness
By bringing a kind of overmental creation
With the descent of each Godhead on earth without
  exception.
Through her word of creation, like Brahma, in the
  matter
She brought the Superhuman reality in the earth's
  every corner.

Sri Aurobindo was happy with the Mother's success
In the creation of overmind and word,
When she thought of a new world with supramental
  access,
Though not the highest truth still poised beyond.

Then came there a downward vision
To conquer the hell of night and bring the heaven
  near
By establishing one Godhead on earth,
With combination of two-in-one
To find for everyone the suitable Supramental berth.

Seven Poems

by Joseph Kent

Seer

Most fortunate in this life is a seeker who finds
the true spiritual seer,
that rare angel offering golden guidance
to illuminate the path, dispel clouds
of fear, doubt, uncertainty

I too set forth in silver grace through cities of the land
    and the mystery
of the way the psychic soul light my guide

Those early flights on the great highway

I learned to glide and toil in the vision
traipsing the Great White Way, pondering mysteries
    of the Tao

And is not the way but a deepening
of the heart, a heightening and broadening of
    consciousness
in the waves of existence?

Wherever there has been an inspiring touch of the
    Divine, there has been the light
and fruits flowing therefrom

And it was after traveling a long time I encountered
    sublime good fortune
in meeting the Divine guide
in the City by the Bay

We received his gnostic light—his *darshan*
at the San Francisco Ashram

"When you choose the Divine, the Divine chooses
    you."

Spiritual educator, illustrious savant, Sri Haridas
    Chaudhuri
stirred our spirit depths, broadened our spiritual
    outlook

The joyous perceptor lifted our being, unclouded our
    mysteries
in an unfoldment of integral truth vision

Sri Haridas scattered dawn seeds as a holy servitor
for the supramental earth

We perceived the "felt meaning" in his lucidity
at the California Institute of Integral Studies
White hair, intense sparkling eyes, the genial master
delighted his group with fables—the crow
who flaunted his feathers in imitation
of the bright colored peacock

"One should not imitate or follow others
to a point of absurdity."

The frog in the well who emerged
to see the ocean

"One must develop a broad universal outlook."

Hours of illumined eloquence from a *Vijnama* seer
who inspired our integral self awakening

All those luminous Sundays
and evening classes in his vision

all those flights in an adventure of consciousness

Appearances

The psychic always prevails in the end and the Divine
Help proves effective. Trust in that and persevere—
then the goal is sure.
    —Sri Aurobindo, *Letters on Yoga*

The mystery of the puzzle surrounded us
in our darkness

Could we ever discover the magic, transmute
the gloss of our elusive world

into earthly delight in the eternal
dance of a mysterious universe?

True, a drear existence seemed the lot
of many on the earth

though ancient Vedic seers had affirmed the world
in original luminous vision

We struggled, dreamed
in the stark reality

The human strife
The misery of the streets

And there was delight!

For they dwelled side by side in the teeming
cities of our world

In the pilgrimage of the journey
we plodded on in penurious wounds

questing toward Fire and the lift
to a better state

And on oracular paths
the conundrum was unriddled, the mystery

illumined in the flame
Life blossomed, transfigured
redeemed in light
We saw this world

just as the ancient seers
as the beatitude

of Brahman, eternal
radiance of the Divine.

Your Light

The world is here to manifest the unmanifest
—Sri Aurobindo

C ling to your dream in the waking world
and the light of your being

midst the dim crowd or contrary time

Employ the tools of your bliss
with invisible help

Sail new horizons in the wind
of the ideal

Hold the fulfilling thought
in the venture

Cherish the ancient one
the Divine

Know thy Self

Unfold the future
in the now

Ascent to a luminous age
in new light

For the new millennium.

Acceptance
for Bina Chaudhuri

S lowly it happens, the marvelous
lifts earth, seeps through

to open sky, changes
world in archaic

shrinking, brings
health

of hemispheres,
continents, mirth

and wonder,
the stars—She

the Goddess
in infinite care

for her dwelling womb

in solar light grieving

The Call

Om Purno Ham Visiva Prem
("I am existence, being in its integral fullness, the
     spirit of cosmic love.")
     —Mother's Mantra

L otuses of light
  on the other side
and here

Urgency up
beyond the veil

The Grace
in acceptance

Critical mass
rising

in plastic
ascent

The descent
in surrender

to blossoming
and release

The Divine
earth.

Epiphany

All now is changed, yet all is still the same.
　—-Savitri

T he candles blaze....

They blossom out of dark
aeons. Is it not the divine
Teleos?

Fire of life ascending into
day? *They* have

descended with gold
blessing, gifts of supramental

light unfolding in our world,
our life,
our moment-to fulfill

the brightest wish
of earth.

Starry Night
San Francisco

The secret of happiness lies in a creative fusion of the unique and the cosmic
—Haridas Chaudhuri

Starry night in June

I climb to the silence
of my roof overlooking the Bay.

Above, the stars....

Galaxies adrift. A sublime
arching over and under
of this cosmos.

And here, this terrestrial sphere—
this earth awaits release

of her silvery realities
to come.

Joseph Kent is a poet who studied with and enjoyed the friendship of Haridas Chaudhuri. He has supported the Cultural Integration Fellowship through many decades.

PART IV

SELECTED ACADEMIC PAPERS

The Role of Indian
Mythology in Cultural Integration

by Viswanath S. Naravane

Those persons who extol the achievements of
modern technology often make the claim that
advances in the means of communication and travel
have "made the world smaller" and brought people
of different countries and races closer to each
other. Unfortunately this optimistic estimate does
not stand the test of scrutiny, unless "closeness" is
interpreted merely in spatial or geographical terms.
Supersonic planes and internet have indeed
overcome the barriers of distance. But have they
overcome the barriers of prejudice, hatred,
ignorance and strife? What has happened to the
ancient ideal of *vasudhaiva kutumbakam,* "The
whole world as a single family"? Conflict and strife,
often accompanied by brutal violence, are casting
their dark shadow over human life in many parts of
the world: in Ireland, Palestine, Sri Lanka and many
other places. Millions of helpless people have been
driven from their homes and have become helpless
refugees in alien lands. These conflicts have not
always resulted from the quest for political or
economic power. Human beings are attacking and

171

killing each other in the name of religion, race and even language.

In this situation, special importance should be attached to any trend in which emphasis is placed on accord rather than discord, integration rather than division and conflict. Such trends have always existed, even in periods of war and devastation. Humanity owes a debt of gratitude to individuals, institutions and cultural phenomena representing the trend toward harmony and reconciliation, peace and synthesis. It should be remembered that the age which produced Hitler, Mussolini and Stalin was also the age of Gandhi and Tagore, Martin Luther King, Albert Schweitzer and Mother Teresa. Apart from such exceptional individuals, there have been comparatively small institutions which have made their own humble contribution to the cause of human unity. As an example I wish to mention the Cultural Integration Fellowship of San Francisco, founded by Dr. Haridas Chaudhuri a half-century ago, which has quietly and unobtrusively provided a platform for men and women of diverse faiths, ideologies and ethnic backgrounds to come together and exchange ideas in an atmosphere of goodwill and tolerance.

In the present article, written in the spirit which permeates the Cultural Integration Fellowship, I wish to draw attention to the cultural history of a specific region, the Indian subcontinent, where significant attempts have been made for thousands of years to create a tradition based on acceptance, assimilation and synthesis. While discussing this tradition, my study will be focused mainly on one of the most interesting phenomena of the Indian cultural tradition: the development of mythology.

Some Unique Features of Indian Mythology

The impulse to create myths is a universal phenomenon. There are many similarities in the mythologies of Indians, Chinese, Greeks, Scandinavians and even American-Indians. Nevertheless, each mythology has its own flavor and atmosphere, its own motifs and symbols, determined by historical circumstances, geography, climate, and other factors. I would like to mention some of the distinctive features of Indian mythology in the light of which it would be easier to appreciate its integrative role.

When we look at Indian myths the first thing that strikes us is their closeness to the actual life of the people. Stories from the *Ramayana*, the *Mahabharata* and the *Purana* are woven into the very fabric of Indian life. Mythology is a living tradition. The study of myths is not limited to antiquarians or sociologists. In India, myths are picked up naturally and spontaneously. If I may strike a personal note, I am often asked about the source of my information when I refer to myths during my lectures. It is not easy for me to point to any texts in which I first became acquainted with specific myths. They have been with me since my childhood, long before I "studied" mythology. Some of them were probably told by my mother as bedtime stories. Others must have been picked up by me from schoolmates, from servants who were like members of the family, or overheard at fairs and festivals. In Western countries, interest in ancient myths is usually limited to archaeologists, art historians and philologists, each approaching them from his own specialized perspective. In recent decades anthropologists and psychologists have also turned their attention to Indian myths. Some of the writers in this field have made valuable contributions and broken fresh ground in the study of mythology. But they sometimes get enmeshed in theories and hypotheses and are unable to capture the richness and color of Indian life and culture reflected in mythology. Some of these scholars have been rightly admired for their dedicated and painstaking work. However, looking upon mythology as "research material" bequeathed by the ancients, they miss the relevance of ancient myths to contemporary life.

> *Myths have been with me*
> *since my childhood, long*
> *before I "studied" mythology.*

In everyday conversation there are frequent references to figures and episodes from mythology. Proverbs and colloquial expressions lean heavily on myths. Even debates in the Indian Parliament, and the arguments of attorneys in court, are enlivened by quotes from ancient myths. These are some of the ways in which mythology brings people together. Hinduism and Buddhism are the two major religions which have preserved myths through stories, poems and discourses. In Buddhist literature many episodes from the *Ramayana* are included, though the emphasis is often different. Here a question may be raised legitimately: What about Muslims and Christians? To what extent is Hindu mythology relevant to them?

174

Today one hears of conflicts between Hindus and Muslims, and of the attacks on Christians in recent years. It is true that an atmosphere of distrust has been created, mainly through the divide-and-rule policy of foreign rulers for two centuries. The British Government lost no opportunity of creating dissensions between different communities. There were also, and still are, religious fanatics on each side. Nevertheless, it should be emphasized that all the major religions of humankind, except the religions of China and Japan, have met on Indian soil. Hindus, Muslims, Christians, Parsis, Sikhs, and adherents of many religious sects and cults have lived there together. Their relations have been on the whole amicable, though there have been outbursts of fanaticism on occasions. Indian culture is the common heritage of all of them, and mythology is an important part of that heritage. Later in this essay I will give concrete examples to show how, in spite of theological and doctrinal differences, Hindu mythology has evoked a positive response from Muslims and Christians. But let me first turn to some other features of Indian mythology which have promoted cultural integration.

Fusion of Classical and Folk Elements

One of the most interesting phenomena in world history is the evolution of Indian culture through a synthesis of Aryan and pre-Aryan elements. When the Aryans came to India, they brought with them a highly sophisticated literary and philosophical tradition in which the Sanskrit language played an important part. Inevitably, there was an initial period of conflict with the indigenous people. But Aryans

175

soon began to assimilate the customs, rituals and beliefs prevalent in India and tried to accommodate them within the wider framework of a common tradition. With remarkable wisdom and foresight they recognized the value of tribal and regional religions based on the deification of natural phenomena. They did not denounce the indigenous inhabitants of India as "irrational," "superstitious" or "barbaric." Their tendency was to preserve, not to destroy. It is indeed unfortunate that the Europeans who colonized America had an entirely different attitude towards the Mayans, the Incas, the Aztecs and other indigenous peoples.

Mythology became a valuable instrument in the creation of a cultural synthesis. If we look at the gods and goddesses in the Hindu pantheon, we notice that the former are dark and the latter are fair. Shiva, Vishnu and Rama are always depicted as dark or "bluish," while their spouses, Parvati, Lakshmi and Sita are fair. An emotional bond is thus created, through mythical deities, between the fair-complexioned Aryans and the dark-skinned non-Aryans. In this way ethnic differences are recognized and overcome. Another way of showing respect to indigenous people is to associate animals and birds with deities. In tribal communities specific animals were revered as totems and emblems. Adoration of animals was part of the reverence for nature which characterized popular religion. In Indian mythology animals and birds were exalted and made vehicles and companions of gods and goddesses. Shiva's bull, Nandi, has a shrine at the gate of important Shiva temples. Devotees offer flowers to Nandi before going to worship the image of Shiva. Garuda, the King of Eagles, is the vehicle of Vishnu. Indra's vehicle is the elephant, Airavata. Lakshmi, the spouse of Vishnu, has an elephant by her side while Sarasvati, the goddess of the muses, has a peacock as her companion.

The worship of trees and flowers has also been a feature of folk religion and ritual. These, too, have been given prominent places in mythology. The *bilva* tree is dear to Shiva, while the *kadamba* is Krishna's favorite tree. Then there is the holy fig tree, the *ficus religiosa*, which is worshipped. The symbolism of the banyan tree, "with roots above and branches below," has fascinated many Indian philosophers and poets. And the lotus, now officially recognized as India's national flower, has been a motif of folk art since ancient times. The lotus figures prominently in Hindu and Buddhist mythology. Lakshmi, the goddess of prosperity, is *padmaja,* "lotus-born" and *padmasana,* "seated on a lotus."

Some of the major stories in Indian mythology are based on the sacred rivers, Ganga and Yamuna, and the sacred mountains, especially the "holy Himalayas." In popular religion reverence towards sacred rivers and mountains is expressed through pilgrimages. Thousands of pilgrims travel long distances to holy places situated on the banks of the Ganges and the Yamuna, and in the higher Himalayas. These pilgrimages bring together people of different parts of India not only emotionally, but also by enabling them to see the fundamental unity behind the diversity of Indian culture. The pilgrim passes through regions which differ widely in language, cuisine, dress, architecture and other aspects of life. But while experiencing all these differences, the pilgrim also feels the oneness of the Indian tradition. Thus mythology, through the rituals, pilgrimages, festivals and other factors linked with it, becomes a bridge between the classical and the popular or folk elements that have shaped the destiny of India for centuries.

Impact of Hindu Mythology on Non-Hindus

Earlier in this paper I raised the question of whether Indian mythology, which is almost entirely confined to the Hindu and Buddhist traditions, has a relevance to persons outside these two faiths. How can Indian mythology be described as one of the instruments of integration if it excludes from its range of appeal sixty million Christians and one hundred and fifteen million Muslims? To answer this question we should look into Indian history without being prejudiced by the tensions and conflicts that have darkened India in recent decades.

Christian missionaries have done valuable work in the area of education and social reform. In their writings and discourses we find many references to Indian myths. The first epic poem in Bengali, based on an episode from the *Ramayana*, was published by a Christian writer, Michael Madhusudan Dutt, in the nineteenth century. The poem, *Meghnad Vadh Kavya*, deals with a battle in which Meghnad, a great hero who fought valiantly as commander of Ravan's army, was killed. Meghnad was Ravana's son, and his death was a great blow to the demons who were fighting against Rama. Michael Dutt's poem exerted a good deal of influence on subsequent Bengali poets.

It is true that in the sixteenth and early seventeenth centuries Portuguese missionaries in Goa and other colonies made contemptuous remarks about Hindu myths. But the situation changed when the missionaries realized that they could not make any headway in India without adopting a positive attitude towards the country's cultural heritage, of which mythology is an important part. Moreover, they found many striking similarities between biblical accounts of the infant Jesus and the myths about

178

Krisna's childhood. Songs about the Madonna in many Indian languages are strikingly similar to the songs about Krishna's foster mother, Yashoda.

Some of Mahatma Gandhi's close friends and followers were Christians: C.F. Andrews, Bishop Chitambar, Principal Rudra and Reverend Stanley Jones, to name only a few. All these Christian friends were thoroughly familiar with Indian mythology. It is curious that while Mahatma Gandhi himself was fond of quoting passages from the Bible and was deeply moved by the Sermon on the Mount and by his favorite song, "Lead, Kindly Light," his Christian friends referred to episodes from the lives of Rama and Krishna to reinforce their arguments. They knew that one can be a dedicated Christian and yet derive inspiration from Hindu myths.

> *They found many striking similarities between biblical accounts of the infant Jesus and the myths about Krisna's childhood.*

I would like to mention here an incident narrated by a friend from Kerala, a state in India which has a large Christian population. To celebrate the victory of Rama over Ravana, the demon-king of Sri Lanka, a festival is held all over India. The festival lasts for ten days. On the last day, known as Dussehra, an effigy of Ravana is burnt, signifying the triumph of good over evil. My friend told me that many Christians celebrate the festival, but instead of

179

burning Ravana they burn an effigy of Judas, who betrayed Jesus Christ. Except for this change, they join their Hindu and Muslim brethren in celebrating the episodes described in the *Ramayana.*

As for the Muslims, today religious fanaticism has become a dominant force in many Islamic countries. And yet it is simply a fact that in medieval India Muslim poets had no hesitation in drawing upon Hindu mythology. Ibrahim Adil Sha, the Sultan of Bijapur, was a poet and a musician. He wrote a book on Indian music and dedicated it to Sarasvati, the goddess of poetry and music. Abdur-Rahim, the Commander-in-chief of Akbar's army, is remembered as a poet. His couplets, which are popular even today, contain hundreds of references to stories about Hindu deities. Rahim lived in the sixteenth century. One of his elder contemporaries was Malik Muhammad Jayasi, an important figure in the history of Hindi poetry. Jayasi's epic, *Padmavat,* has Hindu as well as Muslim characters. The poet, who offers his homage to the Prophet of Islam, handles themes from Hindu myths with deep reverence. He had evidently assimilated the inner spirit of Indian mythology. Among other Muslim poets who looked upon Hindu myths as their source material, Raskhan and Mulla Daud deserve special mention.

Some of the greatest masters of Indian classical music were, and still are, devout Muslims. Moula Bakhsh and his nephew, Inayat Khan (who attained fame as a great Sufi teacher), Alauudin Khan, the father of Ali Akbar Khan and the teacher of Ravi Shankar, Abdul Karim Khan of the Kirana school; Faiyaz Khan of the Agra school; and Bare Ghulam Ali Khan of the Patiala in the Punjab: all these exponents of Indian music selected songs based on episodes from mythology. Some of them began their recitals with hymns in praise of Hindu gods, particularly Shiva and Ganesha.

Indian mythology has thus been a significant force in promoting cultural integration.

Indian mythology has thus been a significant force in promoting cultural integration. Its influence is not limited to India. In Indonesia, where more than ninety per cent of the population is Muslim, the *Ramayana* has molded the entire cultural tradition. The hotel where I stayed in Jakarta, owned and managed entirely by Muslims, is called Rama Hotel. Many Indonesian names are derived from names of Hindu deities. In the famous batik fabrics of Indonesia stories from the *Ramayana* are depicted in beautiful colors. In Thailand, where the vast majority of people are Buddhists, Indian mythology has been a major influence in architecture, painting and poetry. I have seen Buddhist months in Bangkok offering flowers at a shrine of Indra on the way to their monastery.

In recent decades Indian mythology has received a lot of attention in Western countries. Writers like Joseph Campbell and Heinrich Zimmer have written about the significance of major Indian myths which transcend the barriers of geography. It is being realized that the symbolism which is associated with these myths has a relevance for the contemporary world. Many feminist writers have pointed out that the place of the "Divine Feminine" is much higher in Indian mythology than in the Judeo-Christian tradition. Thus Indian mythology is today poised to extend its integrative role from the national to the global level.

Vishwanath S. Naravane was a lifelong scholar of Indian thought and religion. He taught for many years in colleges in both India and the United States, and has delivered numerous series of talks on aspects of Indian culture at the Cultural Integration Fellowship.

Dimensions of Integral Psychology

by Bahman A.K. Shirazi

As human beings, perhaps the greatest task we encounter is that of knowing ourselves. From the dawn of consciousness we have been faced with the eternal mysteries of life. What is this great cosmos all about? Where have we come from? What is our destiny? Who are we? The human quest for knowledge has taken many forms. However, broadly speaking, the search for knowledge has generally taken two main forms: that of exoteric knowledge or knowledge of the external world; and esoteric knowledge or knowledge of our subjective, inner consciousness, i.e., self-knowledge.

Early civilizations seem to have been preoccupied with knowledge of the gods, heavens and the stars. Over the course of history this gradually gave way to the search for knowledge of the Earth and various forms of life upon it. As the tools and methods of knowledge became more refined, we became more able to study ourselves from an objective point of view. In the nineteenth century A.D. much progress was made in biology and physiology, and with the birth of psychology as a separate discipline, our attention turned toward understanding ourselves and our consciousness.

The quest for esoteric knowledge, however, has not progressed in an equally linear fashion. There is much evidence that as early as thousands of years ago certain seekers in India, as well as other parts of the world, made tremendous progress in discovering the secrets of the human mind and consciousness by means of yogic and meditative techniques. Contrary to the development of exoteric knowledge, which may be characterized as a collective endeavor, the development of esoteric knowledge has been dependent upon exceptional individuals who have been gifted with the ability to penetrate into the mysteries of Being and existence. Because this type of direct experiential knowledge is not easily possible to convey to other individuals, as in the case of exoteric knowledge, our collective esoteric knowledge has been rather limited, veiled, and confined to specific individuals and their associates throughout history.

Today, perhaps more than ever before in human history, the esoteric and exoteric traditions are opening up to one another, giving rise to the possibility of a more integrated form of knowledge. This is particularly true in the field of psychology which has developed simultaneously along these two lines of epistemological development. On the one hand, Western psychology has slowly, but progressively, become aware of the value of the esoteric approaches to self-knowledge. On the other hand, Eastern psychologies have become more explicit and available to the field of psychology outside of the historical contexts in which they have developed. This coming together of Eastern sacred psychology and Western academic psychology has opened the way to a new field known as integral psychology.

What is Integral Psychology?

Integral psychology is a psychological system concerned with exploring and understanding the totality of the human phenomenon. It is a framework that not only addresses the behavioral, affective and cognitive domains of the human experience within a singular system, but is concerned with the relationship among the above-mentioned domains in the context of human spiritual development. It is a system that, at its breadth, covers the entire body-mind-psyche-spirit spectrum, while at its depth dimension, encompasses the previously explored unconscious and the conscious dimensions of the psyche, as well as the supra-conscious dimension traditionally excluded from psychological inquiry.

Integral psychology is a psychological system concerned with exploring and understanding the totality of the human phenomenon.

Integral psychology is inspired and informed by the great teachings of ancient wisdom traditions of the world, as well as the panorama of Western schools of psychological thought and practice. It takes into account the importance of self-knowledge, multi-dimensional nature of consciousness and human personality, as well as the multicultural world we live in.

At the philosophical level, integral psychology is devoted to addressing the essential issues of human spiritual, natural, social, and psychological alienation through a profound method of reconciliation of the ontological and the existential dimensions of being in the process of integral self-realization. It seeks to inspire, encourage, and assist humanity in the profound task of healing and evolution toward a future state of existence that is completely attuned to our state of embodied consciousness.

The philosophical outlook required for such a complete vision of psychology is unlikely to be born out of the musings or discoveries of a single human being, or even a single thought system. As the human race proceeds on the path of evolution, new horizons of consciousness, new realities and new challenges arise. An integral approach to psychology, therefore, needs to have an inherent capability to absorb and benefit from the historical contributions, respond to contemporary issues, provide a vision for the foreseeable future and anticipate the upcoming challenges of each epoch of human evolution.

In the relatively short history of academic psychology, a large number of systems have surfaced and developed. The second half of the twentieth century has been a time of tremendous growth and development for the field of psychology. Dominated by both scientific and psychodynamically oriented schools, psychology had previously been shut out of the influences of some of the most important schools of Western philosophy, such as humanistic philosophy, existentialism and phenomenology, on the one hand. On the other hand, Eastern spiritual traditions were yet to be further explored in depth by Western scholars.

After the Second World War, an evolutionary explosion of philosophies and ideas seemed to influence the creation of new systems of psychology, such as existential-phenomenological psychology, humanistic and transpersonal psychologies. In the 1960s and 1970s Eastern thought had either directly or indirectly, through the works of early transpersonal psychologists such as Jung and Assagioli, made its mark on psychological theory. There were suddenly dozens of schools of psychology, like dozens of narrow spotlights aimed at a person on a stage, highlighting different parts of the person, yet failing to cover the entire person.

One of the ways in which the history of the development of Western psychology has been described is in terms of four "forces." The first force is the empirically based experimental-behavioral psychology which originally developed from the adaptation of the scientific methodology of late nineteenth century natural sciences to philosophy of mind, then to the new discipline of psychology. This school of thought has been very influential since the beginning of psychology. From Wundt, the founder of the first scientific school of psychology in Germany, to development of behaviorism through Watson and Skinner in the U.S., and well into the present time, scientific psychology has had a strong presence in academia as well as in the social arena.

Despite offering many contributions, this orientation has unfortunately only focused on the outward aspect of human existence, i.e., on that which is observable objectively—in short, behavior and speech. In this approach human beings are at best objectified as bio-psycho-social organisms and are studied much in the same way as other natural phenomena such as plants and animals. In the second half of the twentieth century cognitive psychology, a recent school of scientific psychology, included in its subject matter cognitive processes inferred from behavior and speech. Since the positivist methodology adopted by this approach to psychology allows only what is observable, measure-able (quantifiable), and testable, the "inner human being" and the subjective and experiential dim-ensions have been largely ignored or deemed unworthy of investigation due to methodological constraints.

Psychoanalysis comprises the second force in the history of psychology. From the discovery of the unconscious mind and the innovative contributions of Freud, to all the depth psychologists who in some way criticized and tried to improve Freud's work (Jung, Adler, Horney, Reich to name a few), this movement in psychology has been greatly influential in the development of both theoretical and clinical psychology. Part philosophical speculation and part clinical observation, the psychoanalytic movement and its later descendants have done much to reveal the dynamics of the human psyche in much of its complexity and to alleviate human suffering and to reveal the nature of psychopathology. Yet this approach to psychology, being primarily concerned with the dynamics of the conscious and the unconscious mind, has not overtly dealt in its theoretical framework with the higher realms or super-conscious dimensions of the human psyche and the spiritual domains of human life.

The middle of the twentieth century witnessed radical and profound shifts in the direction of Western psychology. With scientific psychology disregarding the inner dimension of human life, and with psychodynamic models over-emphasizing the importance of the unconscious forces, neither school in isolation nor in combination seemed to provide a satisfactory framework for understanding the whole human being. The third force, or humanistic psychology, grew in part in reaction to the shortcomings of the hitherto mentioned systems, as well as a beginning response to the influence of Eastern psychospiritual traditions in the newly evolving interface between East and West in the United States. In the 1950s and 1960s, Maslow and others began to shift the attention of psychology from a pathologistic and reductionistic focus to that of an exploration of the higher reaches of the human mind and the undiscovered human potentials and their actualization.

In the mid 1960s yet another force began to grow out of the Humanistic movement. This fourth force, or the transpersonal movement, was a direct result of the influence of Eastern spiritual traditions such as Buddhism, Taoism, Sufism, and Hinduism, on the humanistic psychology movement. Although transpersonal psychology can be traced back to Carl Jung and Roberto Assagioli's work some three decades earlier, it was not until the late 1960s that this movement became popular in parts of the U.S. and Europe, and slowly began to spread to certain other parts of the world. It should be noted that despite the popularity of the third and fourth forces among certain circles of psychologists, psychodynamic and experimental psychology still remain as dominant forces in most areas of the academic world. Transpersonal psychology has undergone substantial developments and changes since its earlier days, yet despite attempts on the part of Ken Wilber to create a comprehensive system ("master template"), it still remains a body of diverse developments without a unified underlying philosophical vision.

The cardinal contribution of transpersonal psychology has been the inclusion of the spiritual dimension of human life into the larger picture of psychological inquiry, primarily through importing and borrowing from Eastern and Western mystical and spiritual traditions as well as indigenous traditions from around the world. Despite the emphasis by humanistic psychologists on higher values, human potentials, and self-actualization process, issues of ego transcendence and higher states of consciousness did not occupy as prominent a place in humanistic psychology as it has with transpersonal psychologists.

> *The cardinal contribution of transpersonal psychology has been the inclusion of the spiritual dimension of human life into the larger picture of psychological inquiry.*

On the one hand, transpersonal psychology is rooted in the humanistic tradition and inspired by existential/phenomenological psychology, and to some extent depth psychologies such as analytical psychology and psychosynthesis. On the other hand, it derives inspirations and insights from Eastern spiritual traditions. Most transpersonal psychologists have adopted at least one Eastern tradition (mostly Buddhism) and have incorporated or fused their teachings with those of Western psychological disciplines in which they have been trained.

One important weakness of transpersonal psychology is its relative disregard for cross-cultural issues. Pedersen (1998) has suggested that cross-cultural psychology is so significant a factor in the future developments of psychology that it should have been called the fourth force. It must be noted here that transpersonal psychology, despite its openness to Eastern esoteric teachings and its international appeal, still remains largely a Western phenomenon best suited to Westerners or others with a Western mindset. It is most appealing to Westerners alienated from other schools of psychology and interested in integrating psychology with one or more Eastern psychospiritual disciplines.

Integral psychology is arguably the next development in the current history of psychology. Although it may not be simply possible to have a system of psychology that would be able to unveil all the mysteries of the human phenomenon at once, it makes only common sense that psychology should cover all the known dimensions of the human phenomenon within a singular framework. This psychological framework for understanding the total human being is called integral psychology.

Integral Psychology of Haridas Chaudhuri

There are a number of methodological possibilities for developing an integral psychology. One approach involves extracting the psychological dimension from an integral philosophy and world view such as that of Sri Aurobindo, the great Indian sage whose adventures of consciousness resulted in one of the most comprehensive understandings of human consciousness and its highest potential for transformation of life. This approach resulted in the earliest form of integral psychology attempted by Dr. Indra Sen (1986/2000). Another approach involves articulation of an integrative methodology and its application to psychology. The latter way characterized Dr. Haridas Chaudhuri's approach.

As an independent thinker, Chaudhuri was little interested in merely reiterating the insights and terminology of Sri Aurobindo; rather he began to develop a system that employed an integrative methodology using insights from various schools of Eastern and Western psychology. Chaudhuri (1973) maintains that "integral psychology is based upon experiences and insights affirming the multidimensional richness and indivisible wholeness of human personality. It is founded upon the concept of man's total self as integral unity of uniqueness, relatedness, and transcendence—as the indivisible unity of the existential and the transcendental" (1).

Chaudhuri's attempt at integral psychology may be summarized in terms of his proposed principal tenets for an integral psychology, as well as the triadic principle of uniqueness, relatedness and transcendence. The following section will briefly introduce and elaborate on this system.

Chaudhuri's Principal Tenets of Integral Psychology

In his effort to explore the basic concepts of integral psychology with a minimum of metaphysical assumptions, Chaudhuri (1973) proposed a number of "principal tenets" that form the basis for his approach to integral psychology. The principal tenets bring together a number of important elements that are in part shared by the humanistic/transpersonal as well as holistic approaches of psychology.

Chaudhuri affirmed the *Wholeness of Personality* by emphasizing that the human being is an onto-psychosomatic continuum, or a spirit-psyche-mind-body unity which in the ultimate analysis, is an indivisible whole. According to Chaudhuri, consciousness is the basic structure of the psyche. He emphasized the importance of taking into account many *Different Levels Of Consciousness,* such as the various states below the waking consciousness, as well as higher meditative states.

He also stressed the *Importance of All Phases and Areas of Experience.* He believed that not only is it important to make direct empirical observations of human experience, it is imperative that all areas of human experience be included in the process of inquiry. Not only wakeful, conscious experiences, but also dreams, non-dream sleep stages, altered states of consciousness, and creative imagination are important areas of research in integral psychology. Besides ordinary states of consciousness, pathological, paranormal, and peak experiences must be considered.

Although human personality is potentially a multidimensional whole, a full experience of wholeness presupposes the full integration of the diversified components and aspects of human personality. Chaudhuri's integral psychology thus stresses the *Need for Personal Integration.* To this end it is essential to appreciate the role of understanding the self, because it is "only by following the inner light of one's own self that the human psyche can be comprehended in its fullness" (Chaudhuri 1973, 24). The *Concept Of Integral Self-Realization* is another major contribution of integral psychology as the profoundest potential for the human being. This achievement requires a thorough integration and harmonization of the personal, the social and the transcendental; of the existential and the ontological dimensions of existence. Unlike traditional yoga psychologies which emphasized realization of the transcendental aspects of the self over the phenomenal self, Chaudhuri emphasized recognition of the self at all levels of consciousness as equally important and necessary for integration of personality. Integral self realization encourages the development of a healthy ego structure and avoids the pitfalls of spiritual bypassing by discouraging shortcuts to spiritual development.

> *Integral self realization encourages the development of a healthy ego structure and avoids the pitfalls of spiritual bypassing.*

Chaudhuri's *Doctrine of Transformation* replaces the kind of transcendence which results from withdrawal from, or negation of, the world. The lower spheres of consciousness, such as instincts and drives are not escaped from or suppressed, but are transformed into desirable qualities. Psychological transformation is achieved through a process of purification and psychoethical discipline. "In the course of self-development ego drives are ultimately transcended and action becomes a spontaneous outpouring of the creative joy of union with Being as the ultimate ground of one's own existence" (Chaudhuri 1973, 3). This is referred to as *The Doctrine of Ontomotivation.*

194

The Triadic Principle

While the above foundational principles are useful in understanding the overall parameters, scope
and vision of Chaudhuri's integral psychology, his
triadic principle of *uniqueness, relatedness,* and
transcendence provides another set of guidelines for
understanding the overall process of psychospiritual
development and transformation. *Uniqueness,
relatedness* and *transcendence* correspond to the
three domains of *personal, interpersonal* and
transpersonal psychological inquiry. According to
Chaudhuri (1977, 74) "Broadly speaking, there are
three inseparable aspects of human personality:
uniqueness, or individuality, universality or
relatedness, and transcendence. In different schools
of philosophy we find that there has been a
tendency to over-emphasize one aspect or another.
It has not occurred to many people that all these are
very essential and interrelated aspects of our being".

The principle of uniqueness may be understood
in terms of two ancient yogic principles of *Svabhava*
and *Svadharma. Svabhava* refers to the fact that
each individual human being is the result of a unique
set of qualities and characteristics that are not
replicable in their exact configuration. Indeed no
two objects or events are exactly the same in nature.
Just as no two leaves of a tree or no two snowflakes
are the same despite similarities, no two human
beings can ever be identical in the exact
configuration of genetic and physiological makeup,
temperament, personality traits, cultural and
historical conditions, context of personal experience
and potential for spiritual development. In this
author's view, the more one understands this
profoundly meaningful fact, the harder it becomes

to use psychological categories and typologies—including pathological categories.

> *Svadharma implies that there is a unique path of development, growth and unfoldment for each individual.*

Svadharma implies that there is a unique path of development, growth and unfoldment for each individual, which must be understood in terms of that person's unique *svabhava*. Unlike some forms of perennial psychology, integral psychology, then, is extremely sensitive to issues of individuality and the path of individual psychological growth and psycho-spiritual evolution and embodiment. It is important to note here that most traditional spiritual disciplines, especially those of the East, have overlooked the individual and embodied dimensions of personal growth. Individuality has often been associated with egocentrism or selfishness, the antithesis of that selflessness which is a basic tenet of spiritual practice.

It is possible to postulate that misunderstanding of the principle of uniqueness results in various forms of narcissistic personality disorders. Narcissistic individuals are likely to believe in their own uniqueness (specialness), but would not grant others such a privilege. Narcissism is indeed a strong impediment to any kind of real psychological and spiritual growth. Integral psychology promotes the idea of a balanced and healthy ego development and affirms the role of strong ego-development in the initial stages of psychospiritual growth. But the ego must first be understood as the *principle of embodiment*. This is quite different from the common definitions of the term ego either as a principle of separation or as defined technically within various schools of Western psychology.

As important as individuality may be, it is not possible to understand the human being only in terms of individuality alone. Relatedness, or the interpersonal dimension, is of equal importance in the triadic equation. Obviously human beings are contextualized within numerous complexly organized systems, such as families, societies, nations and ultimately the earth and the entire cosmos. Integral psychology assumes that individuals are microcosmic expressions of the greater macrocosm with infinite potential for spiritual realization. Just as an individual needs to maintain harmonious intrapsychic dynamics, one needs also to maintain balance and harmony with others and with nature. Integral psychology maintains that unhealthy and lopsided growth in the interpersonal realm is likely to lead to enmeshment, co-dependency and borderline personality disorders.

In integral psychology the human being is understood in terms of both the historical and the transcendental, formless/timeless (non-temporal) dimensions. Hitherto Western psychology has been concerned with the historical dimension of the human being, which includes the genetic/biological characteristics or the physical and vital aspects, the emotional aspects, and the mental aspects of human existence. However, the transcendental (non-temporal) dimension is of equal importance in integral psychology, which recognizes the importance of the urge toward self-transcendence and wholeness. Historically the notion of transcendence has been the cornerstone of Eastern psychologies and Western mysticism. Being so, the terminology often characteristic of these systems has been categorically unacceptable to formal Western psychology. On the other hand, traditional mysticism has had little or no concern with the conventional psychological growth and development of the human being. Integral psychology recognizes and emphasizes both of these areas without neglecting either.

According to Chaudhuri (1977) "the essential significance of transcendence is that man in his inmost being is a child of immortality, an imperishable spark of the infinite. As a mode of manifestation of being, his ultimate goal is union with that ground of existence, transcending all other limitations." However, the notion of transcendence could be misleading if taken in an ultimate or absolute sense.

In an article titled: *Psychology: Humanistic and Transpersonal,* Chaudhuri (1975) critiqued one of the early assumptions of transpersonal psychology—the notion of ultimate states, and the position that transpersonal psychology was concerned with recognition and realization of ultimate states. Chaudhuri did not believe in characterization of mystical experiences in terms of ultimate states. Such characterization, he believed, creates the "dichotomy of the ultimate and the preparatory, the transcendental and the phenomenal….the dichotomy of the lower self and the higher self, the flesh and the spirit, relative knowledge and absolute knowledge, conditioned existence and unconditioned perfection" (9). This problem arises when the principle of transcendence is treated in isolation from the principles of uniqueness and relatedness.

Chaudhuri's integral psychology had anticipated the dilemma of spiritual bypassing, later introduced in the literature of transpersonal psychology. This tendency, especially common among individuals with schizoid personality traits, is characterized by a wish to transcend the physical and affective dimensions through suppression or denial of the body and emotions in order to attain transcendental states of consciousness. It is true that mystical *experiences* attained in this fashion may have their proper place in the process of psychospiritual development. But when taken to an extreme, asceticism and denial of the physical-vital energies problematically become the goal of spiritual practice.

It is by now well established that before attempting to reach higher transcendental states, one must first deal properly with issues of psychological growth and development as well as pathological tendencies and development of a relatively healthy ego and personality. Transcendence, in integral psychology, is replaced by the notion of psycho-spiritual transformation.

The Process of Personal Integration

The concept of integral self-realization is a key concept in integral psychology, which employs a number of important understandings unique to integral psychology. In order to explore the process of integral self-realization, it is important to discuss the notion of self in integral psychology. The present author (1994) has previously developed a model for self in integral psychology which distinguishes three distinct spheres of self-consciousness. These are egocentric, psychocentric and cosmocentric spheres.

The egocentric sphere of consciousness has been the topic of traditional psychological study in the West. Three domains of behavioral, affective, and cognitive comprise the basic dimensions of study in this sphere. Western psychology is particularly adept in this area, with a vast number of theories and applications, many of which are at odds with one another. Much of personality theory is concerned with day-to-day waking consciousness, as well as with what is called the unconscious mind.

Recent developments, such as transpersonal theories, have also included the study of the higher unconscious mind. Transpersonal psychology has extended the boundaries of traditional Western systems by including that which is beyond the immediate ego-based experiences of the self. In this author's opinion, transpersonal psychologists have not dealt adequately with what lies beyond the ego, by failing to distinguish adequately between the psychocentric and cosmocentric spheres of consciousness. For example, the archetype of self as proposed by Jung may be viewed as a psychocentric principle (the soul), or a cosmocentric principle (cosmic Christ).

In integral psychology psychocentric consciousness is represented through Sri Aurobindo's "psychic being." It is quite important to understand the role of psychocentric consciousness in the overall process of integral self-realization. Many traditional forms of spiritual practice have either overlooked or totally bypassed this area in favor of direct union with the cosmocentric ground of existence—a nonspatio-temporal principle known as God, Allah, or Brahman (among numerous other terms). Often viewing the body and affects as a hindrance to spiritual practice, they have attempted various forms of self-denial in exchange for transcendental cosmic consciousness.

Transpersonal psychologists have not dealt adequately with what lies beyond the ego.

Integral yoga deals with this problem by involving the psychic being in the process of self-realization, so facilitating the development of a healthy ego (embodiment principle) and balanced personality. Through the dynamic process of integral self-realization a gradual shift from ego-based to psychocentric consciousness takes place. Initially ego-based personality obscures the sub-liminal psychic being. This condition is due primarily to the fragmented nature of ego-based personality, which creates a dualistic division between the "I" and "not-I" or subject and object of experience. With experiences of self-opening that result from integral yogic and meditative insights, occasionally the locus of consciousness shifts away from the ego and becomes centered in the psychic being. This transition is not possible without med-itative and contemplative effort and is not necessarily a developmental consequence of healthy ego-development. From the psychocentric sphere of consciousness the ego is not necessarily hidden or absent. In fact, from this point of view a deeper observation of the ego-structure becomes possible.

Repeated insights into the ego-structure may bring about transformations of the ego, which result in the development of a unified and healthy ego, which is the agent of conscious activity.

Continued psychospiritual development makes it possible for the ego to integrate further unconscious contents of the mind. As the ego becomes fully conscious, the locus of consciousness moves to the next sphere and becomes permanently centered in the psychic being. This entire process requires the application of the will, and continued effort. It is highly contingent upon the psychoethical development of the individual.

Further development toward integral consciousness may require what Sri Aurobindo called the process of involution, or descent of higher forms of energy/consciousness. This means that the self becomes receptive to the experience of Being, the cosmic ground of all existence. This is also a gradual process. Once the locus of consciousness becomes focused in the Self, occasional absorption in cosmic consciousness may occur. Eventually this experience becomes possible at will. Unlike traditional linear conceptualizations, this is not a final point in spiritual development. A human being may continue to exist and operate as a unique individual, but without an ego/drive-based will. Rather, this individual is ontomotivated.

In short, three levels of integration are involved in the process of integral self-realization: integration of personality, integration of the psychic being into conscious personality, and integration of the existential and cosmic (ontological) dimensions of being. Sri Aurobindo termed the first transition psychic transformation, and the second transition spiritual transformation. These two transformations are not linearly or developmentally connected and happen differently in different individuals. The third transformation is what Sri Aurobindo called the supramental transformation in which every part of the being becomes supramentalized in the Divine consciousness. This would result in a complete transformation of mind, life, and body.

REFERENCES

Bruad, William, and Rosemary Anderson. 1998. *Transpersonal Research Methods for the Social Sciences.* Thousand Oaks, CA: Sage.

Agha-Kazem-Shirazi, B. 1994. *Self in Integral Psychology.* Ann Harbor, MI: UMI.

Chaudhuri, H. 1977. *The Evolution of Integral Consciousness.* Wheaton, IL: Quest Books, 1977.

_____. "Psychology: Humanistic and Transpersonal." *Journal of Humanistic Psychology* 1975: 15 (1), 7-15.

_____. Integral Psychology: Its Outlook, Scope, and Methodology. 1973. Unpublished Manuscript.

Pedersen, P., et al. 1998. *Counseling Across Cultures.* Thousand Oaks, CA: Sage.

Sen, I. (2000/1986). *Integral Psychology: The Psychological System of Sri Aurobindo.* Pondicherry, India: Sri Aurobindo Ashram Trust.

Bahman Shirazi is Director of Graduate Studies at the California Institute of Integral Studies. His areas of scholarly interest are integral psychology, cross-cultural mores and values, and the psychology of Sufism.

The Worldwide Web

by Karabi Sen

The Long Tradition of Connecting

The art of putting things together to create a texture and structure has been a part of our history for as long as we can look back. Nature might possibly have offered plenty of examples in intertwining to draw forth from us this ability. Birds and beavers constructed, and even wove nests and dams; spiders spun webs. It is pointless, however, for the purposes of this paper, to try to determine whether and to what extent primitive arts like needling or threading of leaves with sticks or vines, or piling up to make a mound, were prompted by basic drives, initiated and executed without any part played from observation of things in nature, or were lessons picked up from nature, or a combination of both. Nor is it of much importance to me to try to ascertain very precisely how early in history such experimentations began. I want to start from the assumption that knowing how to connect has been a feature of human history forever; that we have indeed taken pleasure in practicing this skill as evidenced by our attempts at diversification of the arts and sciences and the setting up of standards of excellence in these areas. All such pursuits, without exception, could proceed in their courses of development only because of our ability, desire and need to connect.

Based upon this observation, I want to propose that social practices and institutions are also of the nature of arts and sciences inasmuch as they express the same characteristic need, desire and ability to connect. There are the same requirements of labor, experimentation and insight for an adaptive maintenance of social conduct. I intend to suggest that the cultivation of our social being can yield satisfaction when we make efforts to use our power to connect and remain aware of the fact that whenever we have been successful at connecting, we have experienced satisfaction; that sincere attempts that resulted in failure have still brought some satisfaction for having tried. In consequence, the more assiduous and successful we are in connecting, the more prosperous and enjoyable life will be for those connected. The way to bring about the greatest good of the greatest number would be to keep expanding the web or the circle of connection. Throughout this writing, I will use 'connecting' and 'integrating' in the same sense.

In my judgment, connecting produces satisfaction primarily for two reasons. Firstly, connecting, like weaving, creates a texture. Texture holds and supports, and there is great need in life. Secondly, connecting enables us to exercise our capacity for caring. Connecting can maximize protecting and minimize destroying. If we could think of ourselves as giant rubber trees that secrete gum, then caring would be a sort of glue that we could generate that sticks beings together. Protecting and being protected bring with them feelings of safety, of warmth. The question is: whose safety is the issue, and, therefore, how big does the web need to be? There can be various ways to classify human behavior. The choice depends upon the nature of the investigation. For instance, a team examining a school system may want to classify school activities into the two broad categories of "in compliance" or "out of compliance." A student of philosophy may want to organize philosophical systems by grouping them under the categories of "realism" or "idealism." I have chosen to look upon human expressions as broadly classifiable as artistic, scientific and social endeavors. This does not mean that they do not mingle. In fact, they very often do. Yet they can be thought of as maintaining separate territories with regard to what it is that is sought to be done in their respective realms, and how.

Art seeks to create something beautiful through expression of deeply felt passions. Heightened sensitivity, imagination, graphic memory, well-coordinated usage of words or other tools to be used as media of expression, are some of the essential skills to be developed in order to excel in the arts. Scientific pursuits, on their part, are intended to be directed to things as they are, to the "de-robed," "on-their-own" being, as much as possible. Scientists are aware of the fact that the thing-in-itself can only be caught as imaged in the mirror of our mind, which, with its manifold antennae, bares itself to the outside world, receiving its imprint on its own tablet. But even within this world of half subjective, half objective phenomena, it is possible and sometimes very important to strive to reach a common consensus as to the nature of the object of knowledge, even if that be one's own self; to make that as publicly observable as possible, to have it out there and compare our notes regarding it. Privacy, fabrication, the quality of being pleasing to the mind are indispensable in art. Scientists, on the other hand, have to be on their guard against the invasion of such obstructions and get as close as possible to the constancy of the object through careful experimentations repeated over time, constant verification of statements regarding structure or function, staying mindful of the tentative nature of such statements. We know only as much as our brain permits and only in the way it permits. Other creatures must know the same nature somewhat differently, as their systems permit. We may know what they may not, while they know secrets which we never will. When we come to the social order, we find ourselves dealing primarily with how to relate with other entities.

We know only as much as our brain permits and only in the way it permits.

In a way, our social life constitutes the front and the back yards of our artistic and scientific mansions. In order to be an artist of some satisfaction, I have to walk the path of being a social entity first. I have to experience the pains and pleasures of being in the midst of others, learn a language by means of which I can communicate with others. After my work of art is completed, I need to be seen, heard, read, appreciated. More importantly, I need to continue with my social life so that I can create again. A scientist too lives, i.e. interacts, with his environment prior to, and as his

207

curiosity is aroused. A scientist starts noticing situations that pose problems and calls for answers as the normal course of life is lived. Scientists must further face moral questions to which their work gives rise. Scientists and artists are not prisoners in house-arrest. They do step out in to their yards to work their social being. When they do so, they are not exactly doing art or science, but just relating to others, an experience which they can use at a later time as occasion or material for their art of science. Hence, our social behavior is a distinct order of behavior showing how we concern ourselves with our environment.

I want to include our religious and moral sense under the umbrella of social consciousness as both of these revolve around our awareness of an "other" in our lives. Even philosophizing about religious beliefs or moral choices are social acts for us, because expressing our religious convictions makes sense only in a social setting, actual or assumed. This is true even regarding convictions which are "a-religious" or agnostic. Debating about religion is a way to practice my faith; debating about moral issues is revealing my moral inclinations, even though occasionally I may act differently from what my beliefs may prescribe. My moral and religious profiles are not captured only in what I may do at times, but also in what I talk about as being my beliefs regarding right and wrong, about what I wish I did all the time. My failures alone do not measure my being. Those cannot be used to paint my entire picture. Hence, philosophical deliberations are also our ways to be. Second-degree awareness though they claim to be, they still remain grounded on the same plane of existence as first-degree awareness. "I am aware that I am aware" does not have a hydraulic effect upon the status of my existence.

Philosophy remains an offshoot of our basic awareness of being-in-relation-to others.

Nervous Systems and Connection

Why does our behavior show connection as an essential feature of its structure and function? It is quite possible that this is due to the way the brain operates. Professor J.Z. Young of University College, London, has done extensive research on the brain. In 1978, I had a brief opportunity to visit with him at the Welcome Institute in London. He had just finished compiling a series of lectures on the evolution of the brain. After a fascinating session of sharing of his work, he handed me the publication of his research that he had just delivered as lectures. I had already been introduced to Young's work by my father while I was teaching at The University of Burdwan, India. I was delighted to hear and to have from Professor Young samples of his most current research.

In his work Young suggests that if we try to understand the nervous system as a whole, the brain would appear to be like a hierarchical somatotopic computer. Any such organization would use a mass of information to accomplish a single purpose. The hierarchy allows each level to sort through the information and to use only that part which is significant for the decisions to be taken. Young draws on research conducted on octopuses. He compares the manner of operation taking place inside the nervous system of an octopus to that of an army. Each of the eight arms of an octopus carries hundreds of highly mobile suckers the movements of which, and that of the whole arm, are controlled by nerve cells lying in ganglia within the arm. Young compares the suckers to the enlisted men in an army and their local nervous cells to the non-commissioned officers. The individual arms can also perform independently. They comprise the next level of the hierarchy. They are like the regiments of the cerebral army. There are nerve cells along the center of each arm, which, like junior officers, control them by receiving information from independent suckers. Pursuing the analogy further, Young points out that the brain of the octopus contains lower motor centers, similar to the human spinal cord. These control the movements of all the arms when working together. Electrical stimulation of these centers produces movement of the relevant parts. Young compares them to the regimental and the brigade headquarters. These centers are controlled by still higher motor centers in the basal supraesophageal lobes. Young remarks that these basal lobes have striking structural similarity to our cerebellum.

What do nerves, as agents of communication, pass on? It is believed by physiologists that nerves communicate nerve impulses or action potentials. Such an activity spreading along nerve fibers starts off muscular contractions. In the case of the squid, the action of single cells in the nervous system triggers a particular behavior by the whole squid. Similarly, in mammals, when a monkey acts under training to press a level, single cells of its cerebral cortex evidence electrical activity even before the movement begins.

Young says that the principle on which all nervous systems are built is that of "multi-channel communication." Each nerve cell has distinct function, and each nerve fiber carries only one sort of message and hence only a small amount of information. To effect varied behavior, the system would need fibers in large numbers, each having a different function. Young then proceeds to comment that in some parts of the brain it is not possible to specify what this function is. When we see a color, certain nerve fibers from our eyes transmit some impulses, but in what sense do the nerve impulses transmit the color itself? Young says that in most such cases, "we do not really know what we are saying."

Communication is understood only from a human perspective. It involves a sender sending a message using signals and codes to a receiver who can decode it and take action through selection from a set of alternative programs available to the recipient. Communication presupposes aim and the use of "a code of signals preset by past history and understood by transmitter and receiver." An understanding of the physical changes involved in the transmission of nerve impulses does not give us an insight into what message is being communicated. All we can read in the signals in the codes is that they symbolize the matters to be communicated, relaying the urgency of the action to be undertaken at the decoding end. Young states that the essential feature of the business of living is to maintain a proper relation to the world in which we live. The living system successfully does this by developing within itself little models of those features of the environment to which it must relate. Young has the fascinating idea that our sense organs have come to represent the environment in which we live. This idea also finds expression in Konrad Lorenz's *Behind the Mirror*. What this thinking suggests is that our sense organs develop to mirror the environment in order to survive, that mutations may not be mere chance phenomena, as suggested by Monod in *Chance and Necessity*. This is not to suggest that there is a conscious agent within the system deliberately shaping the models to match the environment. But it does lead one to think that the forces of nature work on our body and leave their imprint on it in the same manner as they do on rocks and sand or anything else in nature.

> *The limits of our knowledge cannot be made the measures of how things are or how they happen.*

It is also very important to keep in mind the vastness of the range within which awareness operates. There probably is no solid line that separates the conscious from the unconscious, the living from the nonliving. The grayness of the areas of transition signifies only the inadequacy of our current knowledge, not the reality of their being. The limits of our knowledge cannot be made the measures of how things are or how they happen. For when we do so, we are in danger of abandoning our pursuit of expanding the boundaries of knowledge, of locking ourselves in to the small cells of established knowledge, allowing what thrives outside the secure walls to assume a mysterious, supernatural, miraculous existence. To have a truly open mind in regard to knowledge is to look upon the field of knowledge as a vast unending stretch on which we are but travelers, ever entering newer zones, which in turn, leads us on to as yet unexplored horizons. We connect as we travel, we internet as we proceed. The

Worldwide Web is never to be a finished product that will not web in any more data.

The Individual and the World

To substantiate his theory about bodies developing within models of the world outside, Young discusses the case of cephalopods and how they relate to gravity. Cephalopods have within themselves parts, the physical structure of which symbolize gravity and movement. The cephalopod statocyst has within it a little stone hanging upon sensory hairs. Action potentials are sent through these hairs. The patterns of these action potentials symbolize the position of the animal in relation to gravity. The nerve fibers are connected in such a way as to ensure that the different muscles pull precisely to the correct extent to hold the animal upright, a function which is lost if the statocyst is destroyed. In the human situation, the three semicircular canals in our ears serve to represent angular accelerations in the three planes of space.

The crucial thing to remember about these models is that they represent not only the features of the world, but also the actions that the animals must perform to be alive. As Young says, "The models in the human brain are not static pictures, they are the written plans and programs for action." He explains that these plans of action do not have to be learned, but are "written into the inherited wiring pattern." The recording of past experiences constitutes a program of behavior that will be right for the future. This process of writing appropriate plans of action is a selective process. Layers of nerves which act as feature detectors sense out relevant information from the world. These data then become a literal map of outside events, from which certain features are selected and recorded by the brain as programs get written for future actions. Such selection involves the use of principles which reduce the number of possible behavioral responses.

The standard by reference to which actions are selected or eliminated are set by the genes, by "the historical information encoded in the DNA." For instance, to begin with, the octopus can react positively or negatively to a symbol. But his experience makes him react in only one way. A signal cannot have at once good and not-good meaning to it. Each switching of neuronal pathways constitutes a unit of memory or mnemon. In general, pain systems produce aversive responses. Such learning is possible only when nerve impulses, which act or are the signals of results of action, reach the appropriate parts of the brain. Nerve impulses thus are symbolic in such cases of internal states which are either helpful or unhelpful for survival. The anatomy of the octopus, and also that of the vertebrates, reveals special patterns of connection that allow these signals to relate to those coming from the environment. The visual and touch memory systems of the octopus have lobes in which this interaction can take place. The resulting product in both cases then passes through a further lobe that has an abundance of very small cells (the vertical or subfrontal lobes). Young remarks that many lines of investigation have shown that these lobes are involved in the process of recording in the memory, although not absolutely essential for that purpose. Their main function seems to be to restrain the organism from behaving in a self-destructive manner. The electron microscope reveals that the very minute cells in these lobes are packed with synaptic vesicles, although the manner of their operation is largely unknown.

Young suggests that if learning consists in increasing the probability of correct responses when the symbols calling for action appear, then having inhibitory systems that restrain other responses is also a necessary factor in learning. He thinks that the prefrontal lobes have this inhibitory function. Young thinks that in the case of human beings, the prefrontal roles might have a restraining function, even in such complicated performances as effective speech in social contexts. Our brains, like the brains of the octopus, must have reference systems to read which programs of action are likely to become conducive to maintaining life. Research shows that there are sets of aminergic pathways going upward to the hypothalamus, the limbic system and the frontal cortex, from centers in the medulla. Young believes that the reference signals that come from these pathways and the hypothalamus "provide the aims and objectives of our lives and the course of our learning". Although in the human situation, crude rewards and punishments like those of taste and pain do not always work, motivations which are more subtle are still seen as incentives to live our lives in a desirable way. Young believes that, despite the still controversial nature of the experiments in the area, we are approaching understanding the nature and place of symbols in the learning process. At last, we are beginning to see the physiological counterparts of life's values, the symbolic signs "which are used to give symbolic significance to the signals we receive from the outside world."

Networking

Networking is a constant affair inside the brain. It is also a constant process that goes on between the

215

brain and the world in which it finds itself. Such connecting never ceases, and the web just keeps getting bigger. This web is not the becoming of an all-engulfing mind, which devours each existent as it continues onwards in its knowing process—a mind in which all exist as ideas, a mind in which to be is to be perceived. This circle develops due to the discovery of a kinship between the existents. It is based upon the tearing down of walls. The world flows into us through our porous being, and a richer flow emerges out of our being. It is impossible to draw a line between the self and the environment, or between the various selves, or the various orders of being, in such a manner as to force these to remain isolated like the Leibnitzian Monads. Differences and distinctions are maintained and respected only for the intrinsic good of the many thus differentiated. To treat the boundaries as solid walls is to forget that the purpose of a house is to provide one roof to the many rooms inside it, the same rooms that provide privacy. Each room has a spirit of its own. At the same time, each room has an entry into common living spaces, which all inhabit together, thereby claiming to live in the same house. Yet so often in life we deny or remain oblivious of our thousand links to the rest of the world. We think we are what "they" are not, and "they" are what we are not. We live, "they" do not. We think, "they" do not. We have rights over "them." We have power over "them." A system of ethics develops that allows the use of one group of existents as means to serve the interests of another. Not that the ecosystem does not operate on the principle of one existent surviving by means of another. But to act in such a way as to destroy the sense of mutual support and dependence that the system really speaks of, to have no respect for that which we live by, is morally degenerate.

216

Hunting as a game is an example; spilling industrial waste in natural bodies of water is another. Fur coats, burning cats to make perfumes, to not recycle paper, slavery, war, monopoly business, unpaid and underpaid work, are all examples of self-expression through denial of the same right to another. If such practices are prompted by ignorance, then the status of that ignorance is avidya or false knowledge. It is not maya or existential ignorance. The latter is a conditioned way of being, under the influence of which thinking and acting as though we were all different is an inescapable way of being for us. Hatred and exploitation, however, are not inescapable features of this thinking. Finite lives can be lived with moderation, humility, active altruism and enjoyment. Avidya is escapable. It is not a necessary and hence unavoidable manifestation of finitude.

It is impossible to draw a line between the self and the environment, or between the various selves, or the various orders of being.

Not only is separatism escapable, but its "other"—integralism and fellowship—may quite possibly be the natural way to be. To be finite, to be limited by other presences, to have some sense of a unique self-identify, does not exclude ideas of reciprocity, unilateral sacrifice, meaningful and satisfying friendships based on equality. Passive letting be, or active caring, may in fact be biologically-rooted behavior.

Sociobiology is a systemic study of the biological basis of moral behavior. The aim of sociobiology is not to de-ethicize human behavior, but to discover ethical behavior in the non-human world. It is an attempt to find our links to the rest of nature.

Altruistic Behavior and Choice

Altruistic behavior is a prime example of moral behavior in human beings. Such behavior has been defined as trying to promote the cause of another at one's own cost. The nonhuman world has ample examples of altruism in this sense. Phenomena like warning calls, fighting to defend one's offspring or one's kind, or even some being of a different specifies, sharing of food, helping the injured (observable even amongst roaches and ants), restraint towards the defeated, are some examples of altruistic behavior. Such behavior is generally grouped as kin-altruistic behavior. Kin-altruism is defined as the genetically based tendency to help one's own relations. In the expanded sense, it can apply to behavior towards extended families, one's own species, and even beyond that limit. Kin-altruism survives as an evolutionary strategy because of reciprocity, a "Do unto others as you would that they should do unto you." Kin-altruism is said to be genetically based. In the biological language, altruism translates into the mechanism by which the DNA multiplies itself through a network of relatives. But are we selfish if we care only for our own genes? We would be if we were intelligent enough to debate the issue and yet did not care to expand the circle: from family to nation, to species, to all life, to all nature. If we would continue to turn our backs to such expansion and still call a structure of wood and bricks our beloved home, and a stretch of land bounded by some inanimate border our homeland, being fully prepared to kill or be killed on account of it. Peter Singer says, in *The Expanding Circle*, that the only stopping place for the expansion of altruism is the point at which all whose welfare can be influenced by our acts are included within the circle of altruism. One even needs to consider the question, if destroying mountains and oceans is wrong-in-itself apart from the consequences on those beings that depend on such environment.

Choice is said to be a deciding factor in determining the ethical versus non-ethical quality of a behavior. If we see that it is possible to expand the circle, we then are confronted with a choice either to do it or not to do it. When we make the choice to do it, we usually do so because we think we are under a moral obligation to do what we think is the right choice. How genuine then is the choice factor for a conscientious person? For willful rejection of the right response, too, there are always reasons why we do so, even if that be impulsiveness or just malice. Our actions are always guided by some reason, whether it be the apparent reasonableness of the response, or the logic of obstinacy of whim. Do animals experience any choice? We can never tell exactly, but they certainly appear to be choosy on occasions. They show preferences. They make rejections. Their rejections can be rigid, or over time they may get over the rigidity. Assuming, however, that there is minimal choice present in their behavior, could their behavior still be called moral? To me, there is more to moral behavior than choice guided by conscious reasoning. There is love, caring, concern, willingness to sacrifice, the felt joy of sacrifice, the grief of having failed to protect, the remorse from a missed opportunity to offer help. Feelings of jealousy, rage, avarice, hatred also have to make their appearance to make the bittersweet world of morality take shape. Like all other types of our behavior, the ethical quality of behavior also admits of variety of kind and degree. Whether or not I should sue my employer is a different kind of moral dilemma than whether or not I should risk my life right now to save a person from certain death. Different resources will be drawn upon to resolve the different cases. If a soldier dying for his country is a hero, then so is an animal fighting and dying to protect its group. If loving your enemy is a virtue, then a dog sharing its food with a cat, or enjoying being playful with a bird, is very virtuous. It is being good, kind, patient, generous.

Animals manifest choice in varying degrees in the selection of food. They display likes and dislikes for people or places. Animals may not know they are exercising choice, but so many times, neither do we. That we have a choice becomes clear to us only later. Acting, explaining my act, and defending my act, are certainly different operations, but there is nothing that is especially godly about the latter two. It is always the act that we condemn or uphold, seek to prevent or promote, punish or reward. Besides, what reason is there to think that the reasoning process does not have a biological root? Choice is a biological phenomenon, and so is reason. Singer seems to suggest that "reasoning beings" are not bound to do what makes evolutionary sense. For example, the use of contraceptives goes against reproduction, a vital factor in evolutionary success. However, there is a chance that the users may be wiped out by the non-users, for the latter will multiply. Singer offers the remediation that the non-users can be educated and persuaded to become users.

> *To me, there is more to moral*
> *behavior than choice guided by*
> *conscious reasoning. There is love.*

But reason is a many-headed dragon. So many reasons can come to the forefront which will tell why to be a non-user is more in self-interest. Singer is creating a false issue here. Ethical progress does not depend on combating the process of evolution. Even if the capacity to expand the circle depended on reason alone, that does not prove that reasoning has no biological basis, that it does not admit of degrees, and that it is nonexistent in the animal world. Besides, reasoning is not the only motivation for altruistic behavior. Genuine compassion remains a most powerful motive. Remember St. Paul: "If I speak in the tongue of men and of angels, but have not love, I am only a resounding gong or a clanging cymbal. If I have the gift of prophesy and can fathom all mysteries and all knowledge, and if I have a faith that can move mountains, but have not love, I am nothing. If I give all I possess to the poor and surrender my body to the flames, but have not love, I gain nothing."

An Interrelated World

In *The Nature of the Beast*, Stephen Clark offers many interesting arguments and examples to prove animal intelligence. It is often said that what appears to be intelligent behavior among animals is really only instinctual in the sense of being mechanical. However, Clark very rightfully points out that the problem-solving ability of intelligence could not function without a sturdy foundation of instinctual perceptions and techniques. Good driving, like good math, is possible, only because the basic skills have been mastered so well that they have become like seeing and hearing, automatic aids ready to assist at the moment of need. Animals are given to repeat the same movement to solve a problem. If it does not work, they act confused. It is said that human beings have the higher intelligence to strike a new path. But acting randomly may also mean that one is trying to find a new path. Neither does acting confused mean lack of intelligence. Rats have been said to be stupid for declining new but nutritious food. Birds do the same. So do people. This is not stupidity, but a programmed fear of novelty. A wasp seals its nest even when its eggs may have been stolen. This may appear stupid or mechanical. But Clark legitimately asks if we really know why the wasp acts this way? When we treat pictures like people, we do not call ourselves stupid. Clark also points out that feelings involve beliefs. Anger involves the belief that one has been wronged. If dogs can get angry, they must have some implicit beliefs. Clark tends to think that each species has its own intelligence. Language is an expression of intelligence and, in turn helps develop intelligence. Animals have language, and their language is heavily context-oriented. Their language shows logical abilities and some powers of abstraction. Clark even debates the denial of freedom to beasts. If to be free means to be unpredictable, then animals display enough of random behavior. If it means choice, then it would be unreasonable to deny them the experience of freedom simply because they have a relatively limited range of options or of territory in nature.

There is no reason to believe that self-awareness belongs to people alone and not to other animals, even amniota.

Clark further examines the concept of selfhood. Selfhood, he says, is a social concept. To be aware of myself as myself is to enter a social nexus wherein things and deeds are attributed to me by others and I do the same to them. He maintains that there is no reason to believe that self-awareness belongs to people alone and not to other animals, even amniota. He thinks animals and children might very well have a preverbal concept of being beings distinct from others and from the environment. According to Clark, we have a sense of things long before we understand them. I can use the concept of moral accountability long before I can consider what such a thing might be. The normal state of most of us is this: to know quite well what we do not understand. Animals show a sense of how they move through a relatively stable environment in their day-to-day life. They are able to recognize and relocate. Hardly any animal wanders quite at random through the world. Most can distinguish between the world through which they move and their own selves. They can identify places, things and other animals. Some monkeys can identify not only their own child's cry, but also whose child is crying. They will look at the mother whose child is crying. Territorial behavior, too, shows self-awareness, particularly of rights of possession or claims. It even demands respect for claims. Squirrels will sometimes pretend to ignore a thing they like in order to sneak back to it later, showing a temporary restraint for the sake of enjoyment later. Clark makes the very real point that as animals live in a changing environment, they cannot rely on a stereotyped behavior. They must learn from changes. They too have flashes of realization that lead them to new responses. They flee from sudden situations that threaten impending death, like a forest fire or a flood. They develop immunities.

The animal-human divide is as much a myth, as is the notion of a purely spiritual culture that has no biological basis. It is based upon a false separation of the mindless body and the bodiless spirit. Singer's idea that only people, through their ability for higher reasoning, are able to perform the "feat" of expanding the circle is not true. For actual expansion we need love. Reasoning helps, but it must be either preceded or followed by the felt power of affection. Animals are certainly able to give and receive affection, even across the limits of their own species. In fact, as Clark point outs, concern for one's own good is a sophisticated attitude. Altruism is a less complicated concept than egoism and may not serve as a divide between people and animals. Instead of looking for divides, let us look for what we share. Male hummingbirds allow their

females access to food only on the condition of sex. This may appear to have some resemblance to prostitution or even marriage, in some cases. Again, is chastity such a big spiritual value that sets us off from our fellow animal females? We should perhaps think twice about it. Human females may remain permanently receptive to the same male for the sake of keeping a stable male around through the years of child rearing. And what about the glory and honor accorded to the mother? Don't we share that with the rest of the mammals? All mammals show the female as the primary parent and the mother-child bond as the primary bond. If we are really for expanding the circle into a world wide web, this insight into the cult of mother-worship should bring us the peace and joy of fellowship instead of shame, embarrassment or anger. The famous words of Stephen Clark are: "If we can remember that we are animals, we may step a little closer to humane society." I would add, that this is also the way to get closer to the establishment of a citizenship of the world, which needs to be the required minimum now, living in the age of space science as we do. We know that the stars are as numerous as the grains of sand in all the beaches that we have. We no longer think, but know, that life exists in many different forms, in many different quarters of the universe. How are we going to cope with this knowledge if we are not able to look with friendly eyes at what our own mother earth cradles?

This picture (above) of a lava beach was taken by the author at Punaluu, the Big Island, Hawaii, October, 2000. Punaluu is famous for turtles who bask in the sun on the lava beach. The lava by the beach, with its slope and the symmetrical cracks on the back of the slope, offers a perfect camouflage for the basking turtles, going to support the Darwinian hypothesis of natural selection. The question is, did the turtle get its characteristic shell by accidental mutations, or by the same natural process that shaped the lava beach? If the latter, then this could be seen as an example of how animals or living forms develop models that match the environment, so helping survival. The process can be as mindless as in this case, which appears to be a sheer interplay of natural forces, or it can be as conscious as the learning of language to make sense of what is going on in the environment. The crust and the kernel that we are, are not unrelated to *where* we are.

Karabi Sen was born in India, but for many years she has maintained her professional and family life in both India and the United States. In both nations she is a distinguished professor in several universities, while guiding her children through advanced academic programs in California.